Reforming Federal Regulation

ROBERT E. LITAN AND
WILLIAM D. NORDHAUS

Yale University Press

NEW HAVEN AND LONDON

Published with the assistance of the Samuel W. Meek
Publication Fund.

Designed by James J. Johnson
and set in Times Roman type by
Northeast Typographic Services,
Meriden, CT.
Printed in the United States of America by
Vail-Ballou Press, Binghamton, N.Y.

Library of Congress Cataloging in Publication Data

Litan, Robert E., 1950–
  Reforming Federal Regulation.

  Includes index.
    1. Trade regulation—United States. 2. Administrative
procedure—United States. I. Nordhaus, William D.
II. Title.
KF1600.L57   1983   342.73′066   83–3622
ISBN 0–30–03045–2   347.30266

10 9 8 7 6 5 4 3 2 1

Contents

Acknowledgments

The ideas behind this book arose when we served on President Carter's Council of Economic Advisers from 1977 to 1979 (Nordhaus as Member, Litan as staff regulation and energy specialist). Arguing with regulators led us to wonder whether there is a better way to persuade them that the resources in the private purse for meeting regulatory mandates are precious, and even finite.

As we wrote the book, we received numerous suggestions and insights, of which those from Charles Schultze were invaluable. We also greatly appreciated the counsel of Bruce Ackerman, Susan Rose-Ackerman, Robert DeFina, George Eads, Robert Haveman, Hendrik Houthakker, Alfred E. Kahn, Paul MacAvoy, Ira Milstein, Roger Noll, M. J. Peck, Peter Schuck, Eric Stork, and Robert Crandall. Research assistance along the way was performed by Richard Kolsky, Robert Lurie, Richard Sorkin, and Mark Steitz. Finally, we are grateful for support provided by Carol Clement at the Cowles Foundation and the secretarial staff at Powell, Goldstein, Frazer & Murphy. Any remaining errors or indefensible flights of fancy are ours.

Selected Abbreviations

ABA	American Bar Association	DOE	Department of Energy
AEI	American Enterprise Institute	DOT	Department of Transportation
APA	Administrative Procedure Act	EEOC	Equal Employment Opportunity Commission
BEA	Bureau of Economic Analysis	EOP	Executive Office of the President
BLS	Bureau of Labor Statistics	EPA	Environmental Protection Agency
BNA	Bureau of National Affairs	ERA	Economic Regulatory Agency
		ERISA	Employee Retirement Income Security Act
CAB	Civil Aeronautics Board	FCC	Federal Communications Commission
CBO	Congressional Budget Office	FDA	Food and Drug Administration
CCC	Commodity Credit Corporation	FEA	Federal Energy Administration
CEA	Council of Economic Advisers	FEC	Federal Elections Commission
CEQ	Council of Environmental Quality	FERC	Federal Energy Regulatory Commission
CFTC	Commodities Futures Trading Commission	FMC	Federal Maritime Commission
CPSC	Consumer Product Safety Commission	FPC	Federal Power Commission
CWPS	Council on Wage and Price Stability	FRB	Federal Reserve Board
		FTC	Federal Trade Commission

GAO	General Accounting Office	NSC	National Safety Council
GNP	Gross National Product	NSPS	New Source Performance Standards
HUD	Department of Housing and Urban Development	NTSB	National Traffic Safety Board
ICC	Interstate Commerce Commission	OMB	Office of Management and Budget
ITC	International Trade Commission	OSHA	Occupational Safety and Health Administration
		OSM	Office of Surface Mining
LRC	Legislated Regulatory Calendar	PACE	Pollution Abatement and Control Expenditures
MHSA	Mining Health and Safety Administration	PSI	Pollution Standards Index
MPE	Mandated Private Expenditure	RARG	Regulatory Analysis Review Group
NGPA	Natural Gas Policy Act of 1978	RIA	Regulatory Impact Analysis
NHTSA	National Highway Traffic Safety Administration	SEC	Securities and Exchange Commission
NLRB	National Labor Relations Board	SIS	Steamboat Inspection Service
NPRM	Notice of Proposed Rulemaking	USC	United States Code
NRC	Nuclear Regulatory Commission	USDA	United States Department of Agriculture

1

What Directions for Regulatory Reform?

Regulatory reform is high on the public agenda. Congress has recently scaled back the regulation of four major industries —airlines, trucking, finance, and railroads—and is considering legislation that would alter the way in which all regulations are developed. Four successive administrations have launched their own regulatory reform programs. Most recently, the Reagan administration has cut the operating budgets of several key regulatory agencies, slowed the pace at which new regulations are issued, and ordered that all regulations promulgated by executive branch agencies pass a cost-benefit test.

Despite all of this hyperactivity, much remains to be done. The consensus that has produced change thus far is only apparent—as with all codewords, regulatory reform means different things to different people. To some members of the business community, reform means dismantling—reducing the scope and impact of the entire regulatory effort. To economists, regulatory reform means deregulating where competition is workable and introducing economic incentives into regulatory programs that are necessary to correct market failure. To many lawyers, reform means streamlining the process by which regulations are developed. And to others, the issue is simply the desire to cut red tape.

We do not share the view that regulation is inherently counterproductive, producing nothing but private sector headaches and public sector jobs. As watchdogs of the regulatory

1

process at the Council of Economic Advisers (CEA), we saw regulation as a valuable but easily subverted tool for attaining worthwhile social objectives. Like army boot camp, regulation can be awful, at times excessive, but necessary. At the same time—as with the military, expenditure programs, and taxation—regulation must be well supervised and managed to be effective.

The main theme of this book is that such supervision and control are missing from the current regulatory effort. Although many individual elements are supervised—individual regulations by the Office of Management and Budget (OMB), specific regulatory appointees by the Senate, and the operating budgets of the many regulatory agencies by both the executive and legislative branches—no branch of the federal government systematically examines the overall regulatory effort and the broad priorities within it. Indeed, no branch has even attempted to determine the aggregate impact of our regulatory programs in terms of either their benefits or their costs. Imagine if that were the case with the federal budget—with no one knowing total expenditures or tax receipts! That is the present state of the regulatory process.

Missing the forest by watching the trees caused little waste when the regulatory agencies were few and their missions modest. In recent years, however, the scope and impact of government regulation have proliferated. Depending on how they are counted, there were fewer than ten agencies charged with regulatory responsibilities prior to 1900; today the number stands at over eighty. This growth in the number of regulatory agencies is reflected in the substantial private-sector impact of federal regulation. As we highlight in the following chapter, government regulations in the aggregate now require private firms and individuals to spend upward of $50 billion *each year*. The benefits they produce, although more difficult to quantify, appear to be of a similar magnitude.

Federal regulation has become a central feature of the government landscape that even the Reagan administration's broad regulatory relief effort will not remove. This status has been achieved, however, in a piecemeal fashion. As difficult social problems have unfolded—the specters of monopoly; concerns over impurities in our food; fear of health hazards from dirty air, nuclear power, or toys—Congress has responded by creating new agencies with separate and broad statutory mandates. To each of these agencies, Congress has delegated legislative tasks—the development of specific rules to cover particular situations or developments that Congress either had insufficient time, foresight, or zeal to address.

The nation's regulatory effort has thus evolved into a diverse set of statutes managed by numerous separate agencies, each promulgating dozens of rules each year. Who oversees all of this activity? Certainly not the courts, which have the power only to review the individual regulatory decisions brought before them. The Congress—through its controls over agency appointments, authorizations, appropriations, and its power to review specific rules—has the potential for exercising oversight. But as we show later, Congress is busy, and its powers are not used effectively. Nor can they be in the absence of an institutional mechanism requiring the *proper type* of oversight. Only the President—through his Executive Office—has taken steps to establish an oversight procedure involving supervision of the development of individual rules by agencies within the executive branch. But the Executive still lacks a coordinated effort to establish priorities among regulatory programs.

We believe that the absence of adequate oversight has major political and economic implications. In the political realm, it has meant that decisions of fundamental political importance—how much the nation should spend to pursue its various regulatory objectives, which of these objectives deserves the highest priority, and, therefore, which groups in society deserve to benefit most—are left to unelected agency officials or not decided at all. From an economic perspective, the absence of a workable oversight process has led to inefficiency, since agencies have been given little or no incentive to balance regulatory costs and objectives against each other and thus to require private dollars to be spent first on those programs producing the greatest benefits.

Drawing on these views, our approach is to examine federal regulation in the context of its economic impact rather than of the legal stance from which it has customarily been analyzed. From an economic viewpoint, federal regulations are akin to federal expenditure programs. Both require that resources be devoted to the pursuit of objectives the nation collectively deems to be important. The only difference is that, in the case of federal expenditures, the resources are first collected through taxation and then spent directly by the government. In the case of regulation, the government orders individuals or firms in the private sector to make such expenditures—a kind of balanced-budget expenditure program.

From this economic perspective, the need for a centralized process for coordinating regulation to parallel that of expenditures becomes readily apparent. Yet, as we describe in later chapters, none of the regulatory reform measures now actively being considered would accomplish this objective. Thus, none would require a *systematic and continuous examination* of the competing national goals sought through regulation. None would establish an institutional mechanism, suited to the competences of each branch of government, to help the nation to set its regulatory priorities so that scarce national resources would be channeled first toward meeting the problems of greatest importance.

How can such a mechanism be established? Conceptually, the solution to these fundamental problems is straightforward. Just as the nation has established a budget procedure to control and rationalize federal expenditures and taxation, the Congress could establish a "regulatory budget" to coordinate and manage the diverse regulatory activities of the federal government. Indeed, if there were a superabundance of unemployed accountants, it might be desirable to integrate *all* federal activities—expenditures, tax expenditures, credit allocation programs, and regulatory programs—into a single "super-budget." Such a budget would enable Congress and the Executive not only to keep track of the cumulative economic impact of federal programs but to compare and trade off totally different types of government efforts.

Unfortunately, the nation is still a long way from being able to implement either a superbudget or even its stripped-down model, the regulatory budget. In the case of the superbudget, although progress has recently been made in budgeting the effects of federal credit programs, the problems of measuring and controlling the effects of off-budget programs remain too great to permit such an augmented budget procedure to be implemented in the near future. The difficulties are well illustrated by regulatory compliance expenditures, which, unlike government expenditures, are imprecisely measured and not directly controllable. The government has no ready way to budget such "funny money" without wholesale intervention into and control over private-sector activity.

The apparent shortcomings of the regulatory budget proposal, however, should not blind us to its usefulness as an analogy—a tool for diagnosing the problems plaguing the regulatory process and developing solutions to these problems. In particular, as we demonstrate in our concluding chapter, it is possible to design a workable substitute for a full-blown budget procedure—a "legislated regulatory calendar"—that requires the Congress and the Executive both to address the broad national issues involved in regulating private-sector activity and to do so in a framework that provides incentives to reach efficient results.

Before proceeding with our inquiry, it will be useful to note several definitions and concepts that will reappear, in one fashion or another, throughout the rest of this book.

We will refer repeatedly, for example, to the term "regulation," a word that is often used loosely to refer to many types of government action, including foreign trade controls, taxation, and even the criminal laws. Indeed, in the broadest possible sense, any government pronouncement or edict issued at the local, state, or national level that is backed by the force of law can be said to regulate the behavior of the citizenry. For our purposes, we will discuss regulation in its more restrictive sense as referring to *governmental legislation or agency rules, having force of law, issued for the purpose of altering or controlling the manner in which private and public enterprises conduct their operations.* Second, it is useful to distinguish between two types of regulation. *Economic regulation* generally refers to the control of entry of individual firms into particular lines of business and the setting of prices that may be charged. In certain situations, it includes the specification of standards of service the firms can offer. Such regulatory measures are most justified when, because of the nature of the particular industry, only one or at most a few firms are capable of using their market power to engage in anticompetitive behavior.

Social regulation, on the other hand, generally denotes regulation that aims to correct a wide variety of side effects or externalities that attend economic activity, including those relating to health, safety, and the environment. In contrast to the more focused reach of economic regulatory initiatives, the impacts of social regulatory programs, such as those addressing pollution or worker safety, typically extend across a wide range of industries.

Much of the following discussion concentrates on social regulation. It does so primarily because the obvious solution to antiquated economic regulation of such industries as energy, airlines, and trucks is deregulation—a point well known and extensively documented in the economic literature and needing little further analysis here.

Similarly, we limit the following analysis and prescriptions to regulatory activities of the *federal* government only. This is not because regulatory activity at the state level is unimportant but because federal regulatory activity is generally more developed and more susceptible to comprehensive reform. Moreover, our interest in federal activities is concentrated in those areas where, in our opinion, oversight by the various branches of government is currently most inadequate. Thus, we exclude from our discussion various federal tax and tariff programs that are designed to influence private economic behavior, because an institutional structure exists to help to ensure that these issues are analyzed and debated by both the Congress and the Executive. It is precisely because such a structure is not in place for federal regulatory activities that the current regulatory effort is flawed and in need of the type of fundamental reform that motivates the following study. Finally, the themes that run through this book are primarily concerned with the design of efficient regulatory systems. By and large, we do not consider the regulatory system an appropriate tool for income redistribution. To use regulation rather than taxation for distribution of income to truckers or farmers is generally wasteful: a considerable fraction of the revenue goes to the wrong persons, and an unnecessary outlay of real resources is involved. In our view, regulation is appropriately aimed toward correcting inefficient markets rather than rewarding particular groups. Where regulation is used for distributional purposes, however, the decisions should be made in a framework that highlights the impacts—the winners and the losers—as is now the case with the distributional decisions made through the expenditure process. We will discuss such a framework in our concluding chapter.

2

Estimated Impacts of Regulation

Before we turn to the main themes of this book—the present defects in the regulatory process and proposals to remedy them—it is worth examining the impact of the current regulatory effort. If that impact is small, defects and inefficiencies can be tolerated. If, on the other hand, that impact is large, then there may be a significant political and economic payoff from spending time and effort to improve the overall regulatory effort.

Below we examine the estimated impacts of federal regulation from three perspectives: (1) the benefits produced, (2) the costs imposed, and (3) the effect on productivity.

Our conclusions are simple but important. Federal regulation clearly has a sizable effect on the nation, producing benefits and costs on the order of $50 billion per year and perhaps more. Regulation is a significant but not the dominant cause of the recent productivity slowdown, accounting at most for 25 percent of the decline in productivity growth since 1973.

It bears emphasis, however, that knowledge about the impacts is highly imprecise. Severe conceptual problems impede the measurement and estimation of the benefits and costs of federal regulatory programs. Moreover, the underlying benefit and cost data are generally difficult to obtain. The available benefit and cost data surveyed below are therefore both sparse and inconsistent. No tracking system for regulation exists to provide snapshots of regulatory impacts over time, in the aggregate or in detail. Instead, we are forced to rely upon a series of studies of different regulatory programs conducted at different points in time through the use of different methodologies. The haphazard state of this data base by itself reveals the inattention given by our political institutions to the effect of our regulatory decisions.

Benefits

The immediate benefits from federal regulation are enormously varied and complex, ranging from lower prices for particular goods (energy, oil, or electricity), in the case of economic regulation, to reduced concentrations of air pollutants, lower accident rates in coal mines or automobiles, and better information about drugs, in the case of social regulation.

For economists, the complexity posed by the wide variety of potential benefits is generally resolved by expressing them in terms of a single metric: dollars. Such a procedure is performed automatically by the marketplace for traded goods and services. Absent market distortions like monopoly power, and ignoring the possibility of differing social welfare weights on different consumers, the incremental social benefit of a particular commodity or service is its price. On the margin, the benefit to consumers of an automobile priced at $10,000 is thus ten times the benefit of a video recorder priced at $1,000, or 100 times the benefit of a TV set priced at $100.

Because, by design, economic regulation is directed at affecting the prices and quantities of goods and services traded in the market, it is straightforward to express the benefits (and costs) of such regulation in terms of dollars. Where economic regulation produces a more efficient allocation of resources, it does so by preventing firms with market power—such as the local electric, telephone, or gas utilities—from exercising that power by raising their prices too far above marginal cost. In some cases, perhaps increasingly, economic regulation also attempts to prevent income redistribution from consumers to large firms.

For reasons discussed in the following chapter, virtually all federal economic regulation has instead *raised* prices of regulated goods and services above the levels that could otherwise be expected to prevail. Consequently, economists have found that federal price and entry regulation has generally produced a net social *loss*. Rather than discuss the impacts of economic regulation in this section on benefits, therefore, we survey the estimated impacts in the section on costs below.

By contrast, there is a consensus that social regulation *has* produced social benefits (although it is not clear whether the benefits outweigh the costs). The precise magnitudes of these benefits, however, are subject to a wide range of uncertainty.

Unlike economic regulation, which affects such market variables as prices and quantities directly, social regulation attempts to affect the economy in nonmarket dimensions. Environmental regulation, for example, is designed to reduce water pollution. But water pollution reductions are not widely traded in the marketplace and as a result do not have price tags that enable economists to value and keep track of them as they can for traded goods and services. The problem is compounded by the fact that the linkages between pollution control and such variables as human health are poorly understood. In short, it is often difficult to measure the benefits of social regulation because both the "price" and "quantity" of these benefits cannot be easily ascertained.

The *valuation* problem is especially severe when human life and limb are involved or, more precisely, when government must confront the question of how much to require others to pay to reduce the risks of injury and death to some portion of the population. One approach is to examine the valuations that are implied by differences in wages paid for occupations with different risks of injury and death. Another approach uses a valuation based on the expected discounted value of future earnings that would be lost by the portions of the population that would benefit from a particular regulatory effort. Still other approaches use average jury awards for lost lives and limbs or answers to surveys asking what individuals would be willing to pay to be exposed to a lower risk of death or injury.

Given this wide array of methodologies, it is hardly surprising that public decisions involving the valuation of human life—or the risk of injury and death—have displayed little consistency.[1] Table 2.1 lists the values of human life implied by various decisions and programs in recent years. The range is

Table 2.1. Estimates of the Cost per Life Saved in Programs
            Supported, Operated, or Mandated by Government

Program	Cost per Life Saved (1981 $)
Medical expenditure	
Kidney transplant	$ 166,000
Dialysis in hospital	621,000
Dialysis in home	228,000
Traffic Safety	
Recommended for benefit-cost analysis by the National Safety Council	86,000
Elimination of all railroad grade crossings	249,000
DOT Cost of Accident Study	480,000
Military policies	
Instructions to pilots on when to crash land airplanes	621,000
Decision to produce a special ejector seat in a jet plane	10,350,000
Mandated by regulation	
Coke oven emission standard, OSHA	7,300,000 to 256,000,000
Proposed lawnmower safety standards (Consumer Products Safety Commission)	390,000 to 3,120,000
Proposed standard for occupational exposure to acrylonitrile, OSHA	2,875,000 to 915,600,000
Proposed rescission of the Passive Restraint rule	180,000

SOURCE: William Nordhaus, "Mandating of Automatic Seat Belts," processed January 1982, p. 54.

1. A useful discussion of the advantages and disadvantages of the various approaches is contained in Martin Bailey, *Reducing Risks to Life* (Washington, D.C.: American Enterprise Institute, 1980).

enormous, varying by a factor of 10,000 at the extremes. Clearly, by selective choice of the appropriate value of human life, most programs that involve human health can either be justified or discredited.

The difficulties of *quantifying* the benefits of social regulation are also particularly acute where such regulation has been imposed to protect human health. The relationship between exposure to certain substances and cancer, for example, is often difficult to establish because of the long period (perhaps fifteen to thirty years) between the initial exposure and the appearance of the cancer. Scientists have attempted to circumvent this problem by using animals that have shorter life spans than man to test for carcinogenic and other toxic effects. But this procedure, too, has its own difficulties, since not all substances found to be toxic in animals are toxic in man (and vice versa), and for those substances that are hazardous to both, the dose-response relationships are often quite different.

The problems are illustrated in table 2.2, which shows the relative potency of different substances in both animals and humans. The six substances shown are the ones for which the carcinogenicity is relatively well measured for both humans and animal species. A common way of calculating carcinogenicity is simply to extrapolate from animals to humans (for instance by assuming that there is an equal probability of developing a tumor per unit body weight per fraction of a lifetime). While such a technique is not completely without foundation, two points are clear: first, there is a wide variation in relative potency among the six substances, with the range in relative toxicities being 500. Second, the conventional assumption of equal potency between humans and animals drastically overstates the relative potency of three of the six substances.

An alternative procedure is to conduct epidemiological tests or statistical examinations to attempt to derive correlations between heredity and a variety of environmental factors, on the one hand, and the presence of diseases in man, on the other. While this technique avoids the problems of extrapolating animal test data to man, it is difficult to isolate a single

Table 2.2. Relative Potency of Six Substances (Comparison of
Tumor Rates In Laboratory Test Animals and
Humans following Lifetime Exposures to
Comparable Amounts of Each of Six Substances[a])

Substance	Test animal	Animal tumor site(s)	Human tumor site	Relative tumor rate[b]
Benzidine	Mouse	Liver	Bladder	ca. 1
	Rat	Bladder		
Cigarette smoking	Mouse	Lung	Lung	ca. 1
	Hamster	Larynx		
N,N-bis(2-chloro-ethyl)-2-naphtyl-amine	Mouse	Lung	Bladder	ca. 1
Aflatoxin B_1	Mouse	Liver	Liver	ca. 10
	Rat	Liver		
Diethylstilbestrol (DES)	Mouse	Mammary	Daughters' reproductive tract	ca. 50
	Mouse	Cervix and vagina		
Vinyl chloride	Mouse	Lung	Liver	ca. 500
	Mouse	Mammary		
	Rat	Kidney		
	Rat	Liver		

a. Comparison based on milligram substance/kilogram bodyweight/lifetime.
b. Relative tumor rate = tumor incidence predicted from most sensitive animal species/tumor incidence observed in humans.

SOURCE: Congress of the United States, Office of Technology Assessment, *Assessment of Technologies for Determining Cancer Risks from the Environment,* June 1981, p. 171.

substance as an important causal factor, given the many other intervening factors that also affect human health.[2]

2. For a discussion of the complexities of measuring the human health benefits of social regulation, see Lester Lave, *The Strategy of Social Regulation*

The uncertainties and difficulties involved in benefit measurement are of more than academic interest. They pose serious problems for regulatory decision-makers and courts in their attempts to devise regulations that balance costs and benefits and plague attempts to design better control mechanisms. It is particularly troubling, as we highlight in a later chapter, that relatively few incentives currently exist to encourage private and government decision-makers to improve their estimates of benefits (and costs).[3]

Despite all of these difficulties, there have been a number of attempts in the past decade to estimate the benefits of individual regulatory programs. Ashford and Hill provide a review of these studies, which are summarized in table 2.3.[4] As the authors point out, these estimates are neither reliable nor comparable, as they depend on different data, assumptions, and methodologies.

The estimates provided in table 2.3 highlight the large degree of uncertainty surrounding the magnitude of regulatory benefits. For example, in the case of air pollution the benefit

---

(Washington, D.C.: Brookings Institution, 1981); Edward J. Burger, *Protecting the Nation's Health* (Lexington, Mass.: Lexington Books, 1976); N. Ashford and C. Hill, *The Benefits of Environment, Health, and Safety Regulation,* prepared for the Committee on Governmental Affairs, U.S. Senate, 96th Congress, 2nd Session, March 25, 1980; and Allen R. Ferguson and E. Phillip deVeen, eds., *The Benefits of Health and Safety Regulation* (Cambridge, Mass.: Ballinger, 1981).

3. One proposal designed to bring some order to the process of estimating the benefits from health and safety regulation is a bill introduced by Rep. Don Ritter and passed by the House on August 2, 1982, entitled the "Risk Analysis Research and Demonstration Act of 1982" (H. R. 6159). This bill would establish a research program for a thirty-month trial period, in which each of the major health and safety regulatory agencies would participate, under the direction of the President's science adviser. Each participating agency would be directed to conduct a pilot risk-analysis study of one of its regulations in order to assist the science adviser in developing a set of acceptable conventions for performing risk analyses in a health and safety context.

4. Ashford and Hill, *op. cit.* See also Mark Green and Martin Weitzman, *Business War on the Law,* 2d ed. (Washington, D.C.: The Corporate Accountability Research Group, 1981).

Table 2.3. Estimates of the Benefits of Environment, Health, and Safety Regulation

Type of Regulation	Lives Saved or Injuries Prevented (per year)	Monetary Benefits (billions of dollars per year)
Air pollution	Up to 15,000 fatalities and 15 million days of illness prevented	5.1–58.1
Water pollution		9.5–10.4 (recreation and reduced disease)
OSHA inspection/ workplace safety (1974 and 1975)	350 fatalities prevented 40–60,000 injuries prevented	
Automobile safety (up to 1974)	3,530 fatalities prevented	0.176–0.706
Consumer product safety	20–90 percent reduction in injuries and deaths from home fires. Eleven thousand fewer injuries a year due to child resistant drug packages. Crib deaths down by 33 percent and injuries by 44 percent since 1974.	
Food and drug safety		0.1–0.3 (drug efficacy laws)

SOURCE: All of these estimates are drawn from N. Ashford and C. Hill, *The Benefits of Environment, Health, and Safety Regulation*. It should be cautioned that many of the figures cited are controversial and may be disputed by other analysts.

estimates range from $5 billion to nearly $60 billion. The wide range reflects not only difficulties in measuring the physical effects of regulatory activity, expressed as reductions in emissions and improvements in ambient air quality, but also differences over how these physical effects should be valued in dollar terms.[5]

Putting these uncertainties to one side, however, there is little question that in certain areas, regulation has produced discernible benefits. Despite the growth in overall economic activity in the 1970s, air quality has improved in several measurable respects. On an aggregate basis, the number of "unhealthful, very unhealthful, and hazardous" city-days in twenty-three major metropolitan areas declined 18 percent between 1974 and 1978 (from 1,985 to 1,637). The drop in the severity of pollution has been even more marked, since the number of "very unhealthful and hazardous" city-days fell 35 percent during the same period (from 547 to 358).[6] These declines in aggregate measures of pollution are reflected in the reduction in emissions of major "criteria" air pollutants identified by the EPA. As illustrated in figure 2.1, these emissions fell 7 percent to 68 percent between 1970 and 1980, the first decade since the passage of the Clean Air Act Amendments of 1970, which required the EPA to establish national ambient air quality standards for "criteria" air pollutants.[7]

5. One of the more careful studies of the benefits of air pollution control was performed by Lave and Seskin who calculated the benefits first by estimating the effect of reduced emissions on air quality and thence by estimating the value of improved air quality in terms of health improvements. Using this procedure, the authors placed the benefit of air pollution regulation at $15-20 billion in 1973 dollars. Lester B. Lave and Eugene P. Seskin, *Air Pollution and Human Health* (Baltimore: Johns Hopkins University Press for Resources for the Future, 1977).

6. *The Eleventh Annual Report of the Council on Environmental Quality* (Washington, D.C.: U.S. Government Printing Office, 1980), p. 147.

7. The reductions in emissions are attributable more to the motor vehicle emission standards that Congress directly wrote into the Clean Air Act and to the various new source performance standards set by the EPA for stationary sources than to the ambient air quality standards (many of which are still satisfied in various areas of the country, and thus are not binding). For a recent analysis of the effects of EPA's motor vehicle program, see Lawrence J. White, *The Regulation of Air Pollutant Emissions from Motor Vehicles* (Washington, D.C.: American Enterprise Institute, 1981). For a more general discussion of the Clean Air Act, see Lester B. Lave and Gilbert S. Omenn, *Clearing the Air: Reforming the Clean Air Act* (Washington, D.C.: Brookings Institution, 1981).

Figure 2.1. Percentage Decrease in Emissions of "Criteria" Air Pollutants, 1970–1980

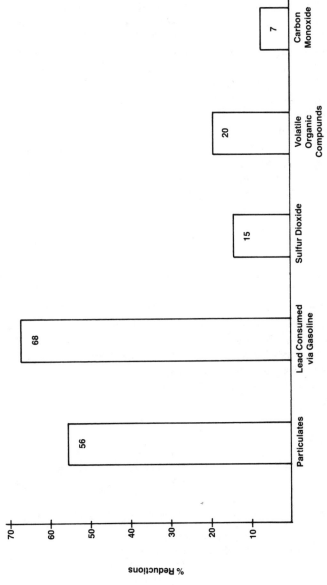

Source: U.S. Government Accounting Office, *Cleaning Up the Environment: Progress Achieved but Major Unresolved Issues Remain*, vol. 1, July 21, 1982, p.11.

Although corresponding measures of the physical improvements in the nation's water quality are not available, the EPA has reported substantial compliance with its permit program. It has reported that at the end of 1979, 93 percent of nonmunicipal sources of water pollution were in compliance with their permit requirements. The record was less favorable with respect to major municipal sources, however, of which only 37 percent were reported to be in compliance on that date.[8] As to drinking water, the majority of the nation's water supply systems now meet national drinking-water standards. However, here, too, important problems remain, as many cities face staggering financing requirements for capital costs for water supply development, treatment, and distribution.[9]

The available data relating to the benefits of other health and safety programs are also sparse. In particular, the research that has been conducted has been performed largely on a *prospective* basis for individual rulemaking proposals; relatively little retrospective research has been performed—by individual rule or cumulatively over a class of regulations—to document the level of benefits that has actually been attained. These shortcomings notwithstanding, it appears on the basis of the sketchy evidence available that federal health and safety regulation has produced significant benefits to the nation. That more about these benefits is not known is a compelling reason why greater attention should be paid to collecting benefit data and to exploring ways that the benefits for regulation can be further increased.

Costs

Regulatory programs impose three kinds of costs: (1) administrative costs of government agencies, (2) "direct" compliance

8. U.S. Government Accounting Office, *Cleaning Up the Environment: Progress Achieved but Major Unresolved Issues Remain,* vol. 1. July 21, 1982, pp. 16–18. (Hereinafter "1982 GAO Report.")

9. The financing shortfalls are expected to be particularly acute in Cleveland and New York. See 1982 GAO Report, pp. 19–22.

costs (or, more precisely, the incremental expenditures made by firms and individuals to meet regulatory requirements), and (3) "indirect" costs arising from the induced effect of regulatory programs (such as the cost of a regulation that induces a firm not to build a plant in a low-cost location).

Unfortunately, it is possible to obtain only a rough idea of how much federal regulatory programs, taken together, actually cost. The administrative costs are the best measured component. While these costs are only a small fraction of the total, their growth over the past decade is indicative of the increase in federal regulation. In fiscal year 1969, for example, major regulatory programs cost slightly less than $600 million to administer. By 1979, this sum had grown to just over $3 billion. Corrected for inflation, the growth in these expenditures is striking: going from $670 million in 1969 to $2 billion in 1981 (in 1972 dollars).[10]

The same kind of precision is lacking for the other two categories of regulatory costs, however, since there is no counterpart to the federal budget process that requires such costs to be tallied. As with the estimates of benefits, the cost studies that have been made by government agencies and private investigators have often used different methodologies and covered different time periods. The resulting estimates also have necessarily relied on data that are often produced by private firms in the adversarial atmosphere of a regulatory proceeding, where there are strategic advantages to shading costs in a specific direction, depending on the regulatory outcome sought.

These difficulties have not deterred analysts from attempting to estimate the total cost burden of federal regulation. One of the earliest was that of Weidenbaum and DeFina, who in 1976 estimated that the total direct cost was $63 billion, consisting of $38 billion in direct "compliance costs" and another $25 billion

10. See tables 5.1 through 5.4 in chapter 5. These figures may slightly overstate the growth in federal administrative costs due to the unavailability of detailed regulatory breakouts in earlier budgets, but such adjustments would not change the orders of magnitude.

in paperwork burden.[11] Although the original study was a useful step, the inclusion of the estimate for paperwork was unfortunate, since the $25 billion figure had a tenuous empirical footing and, to a significant degree, was tied only loosely to regulatory activities.[12]

Once Weidenbaum and DeFina's estimate of $63 billion for 1976 was established, it appeared to assume a widespread and independent validity as a datum. Thus, the authors noted in their study that the $63 billion estimate was roughly twenty times the level of government administrative costs of $3.2 billion during 1976. Weidenbaum has since used this cost multiplier of twenty to estimate regulatory costs in later years on the basis of administrative expenditures alone, estimating that in 1980 the private sector cost of federal regulation had risen to $120 billion.[13] The oft-heard claim by the Reagan administration that federal regulation imposes costs in excess of $100 billion is based on this method of calculation.

The extrapolation procedure used by Weidenbaum (and subsequently adopted by the Reagan administration) has been strongly and justifiably criticized.[14] There is no reason to believe that there is a constant relationship over time between the costs of administrative and direct compliance.

We follow an approach similar to the original Weidenbaum-DeFina study here but avoid the subsequent efforts by Weidenbaum to extrapolate prior results. In particular, we have collected the results of approximately thirty of the most complete published estimates of specific regulatory efforts and have

11. *The Cost of Federal Government Regulation of Economic Activity* (Washington, D.C.: American Enterprise Institute, 1978).

12. Thus a large part of the paperwork estimate relates to tax reporting. Filling out a 1040 income tax form is a regulatory burden in the same sense as spending time waiting for red lights to change.

13. Murray L. Weidenbaum, *Business, Government and the Public*, 2nd ed. (Englewood Cliffs, N.J.: Prentice-Hall, 1981), p. 344.

14. See, for example, "Cost-Benefit Analysis: Wonder Tool or Mirage?" Report of the House Subcommittee on Oversight and Investigations of the Committee on Interstate and Foreign Commerce (December 1980); Mark Green and Norman Waitzman, *Business War on the Law*.

presented them in terms of a common benchmark, 1977 prices (see tables 2.4 through 2.7). This procedure suffers, of course, from the drawback that the various studies cover different periods of time and use divergent methodologies.[15] Nevertheless, the cost concept used tends to be consistent: that of incremental resource costs absorbed. Such a concept differs from the "expenditure" concept used in the federal expenditure budget in excluding transfer payments. In technical terms, the gross costs measure capital, labor, and other goods expended, while the net costs (gross costs less gross benefits) equal "deadweight" losses. Appendix A contains a more detailed list of references as well as a brief synopsis of each of the studies on which the estimates are based.

Tables 2.4 and 2.5 present the cost estimates for social regulation. According to the estimates provided in table 2.4, private firms and individuals were spending at rates from $13 to $38 billion in 1977 to comply with pollution control regulations. Virtually all of this sum was spent to control air and water pollution. Table 2.5 indicates that between $7 and $17 billion were spent in 1977 to comply with federal health and safety regulations. The bulk of these expenditures, $2.6 to $7 billion, was spent to improve the safety of automobiles, but it appears that nuclear power regulation has also been an expensive item.

The estimates of costs imposed by federal economic regulation are listed in table 2.6. Although the list is not complete, the estimate of the 1977 total—$14 to $36 billion in 1977 prices—is likely to overstate the current costs as of 1983, given recent deregulation initiatives in the airline, trucking, rail, and communication industries and the dismantling of oil price con-

---

15. Another comprehensive cost study was performed by Arthur Anderson and Company on behalf of the Business Roundtable. That study surveyed the direct compliance costs imposed by six regulatory agencies—the EPA, FTC, DOE, OSHA, ERISA, and EEO—on forty-eight major corporations. It found that the incremental costs were $2.6 billion in 1978. It is difficult, however, to extrapolate this estimate to the rest of the economy for all regulatory agencies. See *Cost of Regulation Study for the Business Roundtable* (New York: Arthur Anderson and Company, March 1979).

Table 2.4. Cost of Pollution Control Programs, 1977 (Billions of 1977 dollars)

Source	Motor Vehicle	Air	Water	Solid Waste	Total
Bureau of Economic Analysis[a]	−(15.6)−		16.8	5.8	37.9
Environmental Protection Agency[b]					
Private	5.85	7.94	4.05	n.a.	17.84
Total	5.85	8.48	8.89	n.a.	23.22
Council on Environmental Quality[c]					
Private				0.50	
Total				0.80	
Census (manufacturing only)[d]	n.a.	2.24	2.20	0.98	5.42
Denison[e]	2.37	−(10.37)−		1.10	13.84
Weidenbaum[f]	n.a.	n.a.	n.a.	n.a.	8.2
Crandall[g]	n.a.	n.a.	n.a.	n.a.	25.34
Business Roundtable[h] (forty-eight firms)	0.63	0.60	0.68	0.015	1.93
Total[i]					13.4–37.9

NOTE: Superscripts identify sources given in Appendix A for citations and descriptions of important studies.

Table 2.5. Costs of Health and Safety Regulation, 1977

Program	Annual Cost (Billions of 1977 dollars)
Labor (OSHA)[a]	1.1–3.5
Drugs[b]	0.4–0.5
Auto Safety (NHTSA)[c]	1.0–7.0
Mining[d]	2.2
Nuclear power[e]	2.7–3.9
Total[f]	7.4–17.1

NOTE: Superscripts identify sources given in Appendix A for citations.

Table 2.6. Costs of Economic Regulation, 1977

Sector	Annual Cost (Billions of 1977 dollars)
Transportation[a,e]	
Trucking[b]	2.1–8.4
Rail[c]	3.2–7.5
Ocean[d]	0.1–0.15
Barge	0.4–0.6
Pipeline	n.a.
Airline[f,g]	1.4–6.0
Broadcast and Cable TV[h]	2.0–4.0
Credit Regulations[i]	0.1–1.1
Labor	
Davis-Bacon Act	0.3–1.3
Equal opportunity[j,k]	0.1–0.2
Agricultural milk orders[l]	0.1–0.4
Energy	
Oil price controls[m]	1.6–3.4
Natural gas price controls[n]	2.5
Total, economic regulation[o]	13.9–35.6

NOTE: Superscripts identify sources given in Appendix A.

Table 2.7. Summary of Regulatory Cost Estimates (Billions of 1977 dollars)

	Total Cost	Cost as Percent of 1977 GNP
Environmental Regulation	13.4–37.9	0.7–2.0
Health and Safety Regulation	7.4–17.1	0.4–0.9
Economic Regulation	13.9–35.6	0.7–1.9
Total[a]	34.7–90.6	1.8–4.8

NOTE: See Appendix A.

trols. A more realistic current estimate would probably cut this estimated cost range approximately in half.

Table 2.7 collects the ranges of the foregoing estimates into one grand regulatory cost table. The estimates, which are shown in 1977 prices, add up to a total of between $35 and $91 billion. Slightly less than one-half of this was due to economic regulation, and another portion of similar magnitude arose from environmental regulation. Health and safety regulation appears to have been a smaller part of the total cost.

Our cost range for 1977 of $35 to $91 billion can be compared to Weidenbaum's $86.1 billion figure for the same year.[16] From our review, it is apparent that Weidenbaum's estimate for 1977 is in the same range as ours except for the artificial inflation from the paperwork costs included in the Weidenbaum figures discussed above.

Similarly, our cost estimate may be compared to that of Denison,[17] who has estimated that the social regulation he studied cost the nation 1.39 percent of its output in 1975, or $26 billion in 1977. Denison's estimates are roughly consistent with our estimate of the cost of social regulation.

What has happened to compliance costs since 1977? This question is difficult to answer because adequate regulatory cost data over time are not systematically collected. The single exception is in the area of pollution abatement and control expenditures (PACE), where estimates are made annually by BEA. These estimates indicate a marked slowdown after 1978 in the growth of PACE, from 6.0 percent per annum from 1972 to 1978 to 0.7 percent per annum from 1978 to 1980. By 1980, total PACE was $55.7 billion, or 2.1 percent of GNP.[18]

Other evidence indicates that the impact of social regula-

16. Weidenbaum, *Business, Government and the Public,* p. 344.
17. Edward Denison, "Effects of Selected Changes in the Institutional and Human Environment upon Output per Unit Input," *Survey of Current Business,* January 1978, p. 4.
18. *Survey of Current Business,* February 1982, pp. 50–57.

tion was quite substantial during the period 1975 to 1980.[19] Our data come from analyses performed by the Council on Wage and Price Stability (CWPS), which, until it was abolished by the Reagan administration, conducted cost studies of major regulatory *proposals*. These data are supplemented by estimates made by the Regulatory Analysis Review Group (RARG), discussed in chapter 4.

Table 2.8 collects the cost estimates for the major regulatory proposals analyzed by CWPS and RARG during the 1975–80 period. These figures have an upward bias as to actual final costs, because they pertain to proposals; nevertheless, they are probably a good index of the costs of the final regulations, because few of the proposals examined changed materially before being issued in final form.

By any standard, the potential impact of the major regulatory proposals over the 1975–80 period was enormous, ranging between $31 and $78 billion (in 1977 prices) in annualized costs.[20] Recent actions taken by the Reagan administration reduce that total somewhat. A large portion of the projected impact in table 2.8 is due to OSHA's 1979 carcinogen policy (discussed in greater detail in chapter 3), which established certain policies to be applied in future regulatory proceedings involving worker exposure to toxic substances. The current OSHA administrator, Thorne Auchter, has since announced a reconsideration of that policy. Moreover, as we discuss further

---

19. The popular method of estimating the trend in regulation has been to count pages in the *Federal Register*. This is a frivolous technique, however, because there is no consistent relationsip between the cost of a regulation and how many pages it occupies in the *Federal Register*. Moreover, other factors, such as changes in notification and publication procedures, also have an important effect on the number of total pages that appear each year. To the extent that the number of pages of any document provides an indication of the growth in federal regulations, one would do better to examine the size of the Code of Federal Regulations, which shows continued growth over the past two decades, but nothing like the explosion in the number of pages in the *Federal Register*.

20. As indicated in the note to the table some of the regulations were not promulgated or have since been rescinded.

Table 2.8. Estimated Costs of Major Regulations Proposed
between 1975 and 1980 (Billions of 1977 dollars)

Source of estimate	Annualized Cost RARG or CWPS	Agency
Environmental Protection Agency		
New Source Performance Standards:		
Steam electric utilities	3.1–4.3	
Hazardous wastes	4.0–8.0	
Photochemical oxidants	6.9–18.8	
Drinking water	1.2–1.7	
Other		0.26–0.41
Total	15.5–33.2	
Occupational Health & Safety Administration		
Generic carcinogens	11.0–36.0	
Benzene	0.50	
Cotton dust	0.72	
Noise	1.99	
Other	0.94–1.05	
Total	15.2–40.3	
Department of the Interior		
Surface mining	2.0–3.0	
Department of Energy		
Coal conversion	0.8–1.0	
Department of Transportation		
Public transport for handicapped	0.08	
Food and Drug Administration		
Prescription drug labeling	0.09–0.300	0.09–0.30
Grand Total		
Including generic carcinogens	33.6–77.9	
Excluding generic carcinogens	22.6–41.9	

NOTE: The table was constructed by the following procedure. All RARG filings through summer 1980 are included. In addition, all CWPS public filings
over the period 1975 to summer 1980 were examined to see if they pertained to
a regulation. Note that some of the proposed regulations either were not
promulgated or have since been rescinded.

in subsequent chapters, the Reagan administration has recently
rolled back or modified a series of other social regulations,

including the Department of Transportation's (DOT) passive restraint and bumper rules, the Department of Energy's (DOE) coal conversion regulations, and the Department of Education's rule requiring bilingual education. The annual cost savings from these efforts, according to the administration, are projected to reach approximately $2 billion per year. To these savings must be added the reduced costs from the economic deregulation programs, which we have already indicated may save $7 to 18 billion annually.

Despite the recent reductions, the costs imposed on the private sector by federal regulation over the foreseeable future will, by any measure, continue to be large. According to the Council on Environmental Quality, the total costs for the period 1979–88 of all pollution abatement efforts (air, water, solid waste, etc.) are estimated to be *$735 billion* (in 1979 dollars), or an average of over *$80 billion per year*.[21] Although all of these costs cannot be attributable to regulation (since some abatement efforts would be undertaken by firms even if no federal environmental regulation existed), it is fair to say that a sizable portion can be. Since the federal government will, over this same period, continue its other regulatory efforts, economic and social, the total cost of all future federal regulatory activities is likely to be even larger than it has been in the past.

Productivity

The recent decline in the nation's productivity growth has been a matter of public attention and concern. After averaging 2.5 percent growth per year from 1948 through 1973, labor productivity growth has since fallen to around 0.5 percent annually. Many villains have been singled out, including increased energy prices, shifts in demand toward services and away from manufactured goods, and industry's quest for the quick buck rather than the innovative product or process.

Politicians, some economists, and a variety of other pundits have added the effects of regulation—particularly social regulation—to this list. The reason is easy to understand. The benefits of social regulatory programs generally do not show up

21. 1982 GAO Report, p. 52.

in marketed output, as it is conventionally measured. At the same time, these regulations require additional "direct" inputs—scrubbers added to an electricity generating plant or engineering controls installed to reduce toxic emissions in the workplace. Because productivity is measured in terms of marketed output divided by marketed input, the regulatory requirements cause measured productivity to decline. Only in a broader framework that measured all outputs, both market and nonmarket, would output rise, permitting true productivity to fall by a lesser amount or to show a gain.[22]

Regulatory programs also can have an indirect effect on productivity. If a regulatory program precludes the building of steel mills in the most efficient location, this leads to higher transportation costs. In this case, the total costs of delivering steel to industry would rise, even if no direct cost were imposed by the program. Similarly, if firms spent more effort fighting the regulatory process than on innovation, regulation might slow productivity growth.

We have examined recent behavior in manufacturing and elsewhere to see whether the direct or indirect effects of regulation on productivity growth have been significant. The *direct* effects of environment, health, and safety regulation— measured in terms of their impact on productive inputs—have been carefully measured by Edward Denison, who estimated that over the period from the early 1960s to 1973–75, regulation caused productivity growth to slow by 0.25 percentage points per annum.[23] This compares with a total slowdown in annual productivity growth over this period of approximately two percentage points per annum. Although no complete study has been made of the direct productivity effect of economic regulation, the fragmentary evidence that exists suggests that it has been less significant than social regulation over the last decade.

The *indirect* impacts of regulation on productivity are much

22. In a comprehensive set of national accounts using consistent pricing of environmental inputs and outputs, an efficient regulation would raise the net output of the nation.

23. Edward Denison, "Effects of Selected Changes in the Institutional and Human Environment upon Output per Unit Input," *Survey of Current Business,* January 1978, p. 4.

more difficult to measure. The approach we pursue here is to examine whether the productivity slowdown appears more prominent in those industries that have been most heavily regulated. That task can be simplified if it is assumed that the indirect effects are highly correlated with the direct effects. This permits us to look at the relation between direct regulatory costs per unit output and productivity behavior as a way of determining whether industry must not only bear the burden of high direct costs mandated by regulatory programs but must also incur heavy indirect costs, such as litigation expenses, costs related to obtaining permits for new construction, and costs imposed due to the inability to build plants in nonattainment areas. In contrast, the microprocessor and computer industries are relatively free from both direct and indirect costs. A more complete description of our technique is set forth in Appendix B.

Figure 2.2 presents evidence on the relation between pollution costs and productivity in several manufacturing industries. We focus on pollution control expenditures as a proxy for regulatory expenditures in general because pollution control cost data are the only compliance cost data available by industry.[24] More specifically, figure 2.2 plots for fifty-nine industries the ratio of expenditures for environmental protection to the value of the output shipped in 1977 against the change in the average annual growth rate of labor productivity from before 1973 to the 1973–78 period.[25] For instance, the point on the graph labeled "steel" shows that pollution control costs in the steel industry were 1.4 percent of the value of output shipped in 1977, and the growth of labor productivity in steel was 3 percent per annum higher before 1973 than after. Theoretically, the higher an industry's ratio of pollution control cost to its value of output, the more the rate of growth of measured productivity should have declined after 1973.[26]

24. Specifically, direct costs are used as a proxy variable for indirect costs.
25. The industries are the four digit industries as defined in the Standard Industrial Classification.
26. Technically, the correct relationship is not between the proportion of total output value devoted to pollution control and the change in productivity growth rates but between the *change* in this proportion and the change in annual

Figure 2.2. The Relation between Pollution Control Expenditures and the Productivity Slowdown, Fifty-nine Manufacturing Industries

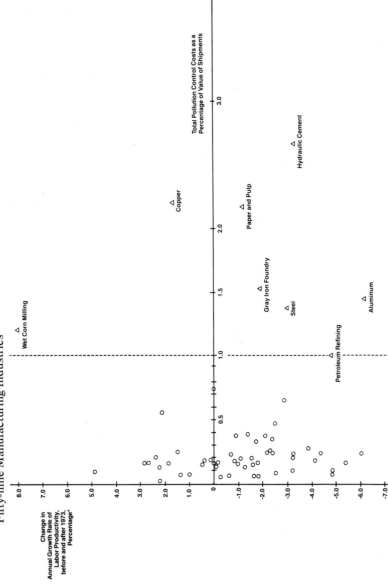

*Vertical axis is calculated as (the average growth rate of labor productivity during the period 1978–73) minus (the average

As indicated in figure 2.2, most of the industries surveyed spent less than 0.7 percent of the value of their 1977 output for pollution control. There is no visually discernible correlation between pollution expenditures and productivity growth rates for these industries, probably because they are only modestly affected by environmental regulation. Indeed, for this group, an *increase* in the rate of productivity growth seems as likely as a decrease to accompany any given ratio of pollution costs to output value. However, for those industries with ratios of pollution cost to output value greater than or equal to 1 percent, higher ratios appear to be related to declines in the growth rate of labor productivity. This observation is reinforced when the data for the two groups of industries are averaged; the average decrease in the rate of productivity growth for those industries more heavily affected by environmental regulation is 1.3 percent.

This numerical evidence is analyzed in a more formal statistical fashion in Appendix B. That examination suggests that pollution control costs can explain but a modest amount of the variation in productivity growth across industries. According to this analysis, there would have been a significant decline in the rate of productivity growth in all industries after 1973, regardless of the intensity with which the federal government pursued its regulatory program. Nevertheless, the results also suggest that intensity of regulation exacerbated the decline in the overall rate of growth of productivity. On average, environmental regulation reduced the post-1973 rate of growth of

---

productivity growth rates. A once-and-for-all increase in the proportion of pollution costs in total output value will reduce the rate of growth of labor productivity for one period but need not affect it thereafter. However, in this instance, the ratio of pollution control costs to measured output value is an acceptable proxy for the 1973–77 change in this ratio. Before 1970, business spent very little for pollution control. Since then, pollution control expenditures have risen rapidly both in absolute terms and as a percentage of the value of output. Thus the level of the proportion in 1977 is a good proxy for the total change in the proportion between 1973 and 1977. Put another way, the use of the level of the proportion rather than the change in annual growth rates of the proportion affects the size of the relationship but not its sign.

productivity in heavily affected industries (those whose pollution costs were greater than 1 percent of sales) by 0.5 percent per annum. For all manufacturing, the statistical evidence suggests that annual productivity growth slowed by about 0.15 percentage points as a result of higher pollution abatement costs after 1973.

Given the economic importance and the shrillness of the political debate about the burdens of regulation, it is surprising how little serious research exists on both the direct and indirect effects of regulation on productivity growth. In particular, the only other disaggregated study to date on this issue is that of Robert Crandall.[27]

Using larger aggregates than those analyzed here, Crandall has analyzed the statistical relationship between the percentage growth in productivity between 1973 and 1976 and the weighted percentage growth in capital stock, labor input, and total pollution control costs. His results suggest that, for the eighteen industries studied, a doubling of pollution control costs would reduce the level of productivity by an enormous amount— 7 percent. By way of comparison, our results suggest that a doubling of pollution costs—from, say, 0.22 to 0.44 percent of the value of output—would reduce productivity growth by 0.15 percent per annum over the 1973–78 period. Cumulated over five years, that annual reduction would lower the level of measured productivity in 1978 by approximately 0.75 percent —or a figure only one-tenth as large as the estimate made by Crandall.

We find the discrepancy between Crandall's results and ours somewhat puzzling. The differences in sample size and variables can hardly explain such a major discrepancy. A more likely source of the difference is the choice of dependent vari-

---

27. Robert W. Crandall, "Regulation and Productivity Growth," reprinted in *The Decline in Productivity Growth,* Proceedings of a conference held in June 1980, Federal Reserve Bank of Boston Conference Series No. 22. The few other studies of productivity generally include H. S. Houthakker, "Competition, Regulation, and Efficiency," in Jules Backman, ed. *Regulation and Deregulation* (Columbus, Ohio: Merrill, 1981); G. B. Christainsen and R. H. Haveman, "Public Regulations and the Slowdown in Productivity Growth," *American Economic Review,* May 1981, pp. 320–25.

able. In our view, higher pollution abatement costs led to a greater *slowdown* in productivity growth, whereas in Crandall's view, higher pollution abatement costs led to a lower *level* of productivity growth. The Crandall specification seems defective, as it uses the average productivity growth of the *economy* after 1973 as the control group, whereas we use the productivity growth in each particular *industry* before 1973 as its own control group. Given the persistence of productivity patterns in specific industries over time, we believe that our procedure provides a more accurate picture of the indirect effects of regulation.[28]

What can one conclude about the effects of regulatory activities on growth? First, there is fairly strong evidence from Denison that the increased *direct* costs of complying with environmental, health, and safety regulations have led to a slowdown in productivity growth of around 0.25 percent per annum. It is unlikely that economic regulation added significantly to this effect. Second, there is some suggestion that the indirect regulatory costs, such as proscription of technologies or locations, may have also contributed to the slowdown. Our best guess is that, for manufacturing, about 0.15 percentage points per annum of the slowdown of productivity growth since 1973 should be tied to the indirect costs associated with higher pollution control costs, which we use as a proxy for mandated compliance costs generally. As pollution abatement occurs disproportionately in manufacturing, indirect costs weigh less heavily in the rest of the economy.

In sum, although the evidence is spotty and some of the relationships weak, we believe that regulation has accounted for between 0.3 and 0.4 percentage points of the 2 percentage point slowdown in aggregate productivity growth since 1973. This finding suggests to us that regulation has been a significant but not dominant contributor to the poorer economic performance in the United States economy in recent years.

---

28. In one respect, Crandall's study is conceptually superior to ours because it uses capital stock data to calculate total factor productivity. This is not possible for our more disaggregated sample because capital stock data are not available. In general, however, studies confirm that labor productivity and total factor productivity in individual industries have moved together since 1973.

3

Why and How We Regulate

The sizable impacts of federal regulation documented in the last chapter highlight the stakes involved in introducing and implementing regulatory programs. Yet, as we have indicated, these programs were not established all at once. The nation's regulatory effort has grown in an uncoordinated fashion, responding to shifting political and ideological trends. In this chapter, we explore the manner in which interest group pressures have influenced the growth of federal regulatory programs. In theory, regulation should arise as a response to market failures. In practice, regulation is more accurately characterized as a government tool for *redistributing* society's resources toward those groups that have successfully enlisted the support of the government on their behalf. Viewing regulation in the distributive model allows us to understand clearly the major defects of the current regulatory effort, which we analyze in chapter 4, and suggests the reforms we outline in chapters 6 and 7.

Why We Regulate

Americans have always displayed an ambivalence about government intervention in the economy, espousing on the one hand the ideology of freely competitive markets but eager, on the other, for numerous forms of government assistance. Over most of the last two decades, the proponents of intervention have had the upper hand as a wide variety of business, labor, and environmental groups have successfully persuaded the federal government to address their own particular concerns.

The most visible way in which the role of the federal government has expanded is through the growth in federal expenditures and taxation. In 1940, for example, the federal government collected in taxes and expended approximately $10 billion, or roughly 10 percent of GNP. By 1982, federal expenditures had reached $763 billion or 25 percent of GNP.[1]

The scope and impact of regulation as a tool of government policy have expanded even more rapidly over this period. The number of regulatory programs has grown manyfold, and the regulations that have been issued affect the daily operations of most business enterprises and households. Moreover, as we indicated in the last chapter, the annual private sector impact of federal regulation—in both costs and benefits—reaches into many tens of billions of dollars.

The large number of regulatory agencies and their mandates clearly are too diverse to have been put in place in response to just a single set of forces. Nevertheless, it is possible to distill two basic perspectives—one normative, the other positive—on the origins of federal regulation. Without describing in detail the chronological development of the many regulatory programs that now populate the Washington landscape, we describe and highlight below the importance of the differences between each of these views.[2]

1. Data from *Economic Report of the President,* 1983. Another, often unnoticed, indication of the growth in the federal government has been the rapid expansion of off-budget forms of government assistance, such as the debts issued by government-created entities and the extension of loan guarantees, which together exceeded $100 billion in 1981. See Herman B. Leonard and Elisabeth H. Rhyne, "Federal Credit and the Shadow Budget," *The Public Interest,* Fall 1981, pp. 40–58.

2. Broad summaries of the various theories of federal regulation can be found in chapter 1 of Bruce M. Owen and Ronald Breautigem, *The Regulation Game: Strategic Use of the Administrative Process* (Cambridge: Ballinger, 1978). See also James Q. Wilson, ed., *The Politics of Regulation* (New York: Basic Books, 1980); Barry M. Mitnick, *The Political Economy of Regulation* (New York: Columbia Univ. Press, 1980).

The "Market Failure" Theory of Regulation

The traditional view of regulation is normative: regulatory measures ought to be used to correct certain well recognized "market failures" that impede market efficiency. Three specific defects have been highlighted by several generations of economists: (1) natural monopoly, (2) imperfect information, and (3) externalities.

The "natural monopoly" problem arises where the technology of an industry allows but a single efficient producer. In such a case, the resulting firm would have sufficient market power to earn excess profits. Such conditions have typically prevailed in the public utility industries—particularly the local distribution of gas, electricity, and telephone—that have long been subject to regulation of both rates and entry.

The second defect involves insufficient information. The efficiency of a market economy requires that all market participants possess the information necessary to make reasoned choices. If, however, consumers are not fully informed about the characteristics of the products they buy, or if producers are not aware of the full array of production methods, an inefficient mix of goods may be produced by less than optimal production techniques. Because the benefits of providing information are so difficult for providers to capture, markets frequently fail to produce an efficient supply of information. Where the benefits of having information outweigh the costs of providing it, economic efficiency could be improved, in principle, through regulations to assure that it is made available. Examples of such regulation today are the many food, drug, health, and energy labeling and consumer-disclosure rules.

The third and most important source of market failure arises from technological interactions between actors in the economy that are not reflected in prices. These interactions —or externalities—can either impose costs or confer benefits on other parties. A well-known interaction that imposes costs on third parties is unregulated industrial pollution. Where producers are not required to pay for the damage to others arising from the pollution, the pollutants will clearly be oversupplied. Precisely the opposite will occur in the case of public goods, such as the generation of new knowledge, police and fire protection, sewage and waste facilities, and national defense. Because the benefits conferred by public goods cannot be fully (and practically) captured by their producers, such goods will be undersupplied by the private market.

It bears emphasis that the existence of externalities does not necessarily lead to market failure. In the case of industrial pollution, if the injured parties are few in number and can easily negotiate with a similarly small number of producers, the marketplace, through the assignment and enforcement of property rights, may well produce an efficient level of pollution. Under this restrictive set of conditions, the assignment of the property rights either to be free from pollution or to produce as much pollution as one might desire will affect the distribution of income, but not the efficiency of the result.[3] It is more usual, however, that the number of parties affected by an externality is so large that private negotiation becomes too costly and inefficient a method for translating interests into effective results. In addition, the damage suffered by each of the many individuals or firms affected may be too small in each case to induce the injured parties to band together to seek redress either through negotiation or litigation. It is in such situations that the existence of an externality causes significant excess social costs, i.e., market failures.

Many different tools can be used by the government to correct the foregoing market failures. As arrayed in table 3.1, these are typically placed in two categories: (1) commands and controls and (2) incentives. The former includes such measures as price and entry controls, the setting of standards, and forced disclosure. The principal tools in the latter category are taxation and government subsidies.

Table 3.1 illustrates the different combinations of tools that

3. This is the famous Coase theorem, explained in R. Coase, "The Problem of Social Cost," *Journal of Law and Economics* 3 (1960), pp. 1–44. This is not the place to quarrel with the adequacy of the reasoning behind, or the general applicability of, the Coase theorem. We would only point out that just because negotiations *might* lead to an efficient outcome does not prove they *will*; witness wars and strikes, which are instances of Coase counterexamples.

Table 3.1. Commonly Used Techniques for Correcting Market Failures

Techniques	Imperfect Market Structure	Insufficient Information	Externalities
	Sources of Market Failure		
Command and Control:			
Price Control	X		
Entry Regulation	X		
Standard Setting		X	X
Prohibitions			X
Design			X
Performance			X
Disclosure		X	
Antitrust Enforcement	X		
Incentive:			
Competitive Bidding for Business Licenses	X		X
Taxes, Fees			X
Public Expenditures		X	X
Private Bargaining		X	X

SOURCE: This table draws on Stephen Breyer, "Analyzing Regulatory Failure: Mismatches, Less Restrictive Alternatives, and Reform," *Harvard Law Review*, January 1979, pp. 459–609. See also *Federal Regulation: Roads to Reform*, Report by the ABA Commission on Law and the Economy, chapter 3.

can be used to accomplish the various objectives. For example, the problem of insufficient information has been met by government-funded information programs (energy conservation), prohibitions on certain types of advertising (cigarettes), forced disclosure (Rely tampons), and sometimes by private bargaining. Similar combinations can be used to solve the two other market imperfections. However, regulation in the United States has typically displayed a strong bias in favor of commands and controls rather than incentives to accomplish specific objectives (see chapter 4). This bias is particularly evident in the case of externalities, which have been addressed primarily through standard-setting, and far less through government expenditures (such as publicly funded water treatment plants) or taxation (such as fast depreciation writeoffs on pollution control facilities). The infrequent use of marketlike incentives highlights the central weakness of the market failure paradigm. If society were interested in regulation primarily as a tool to correct the defects in the private market, one would expect that regulation would simulate the most important feature of the market: the use of the "invisible hand" of price incentives, which encourages but does not command private actors to act in the broader social interest. That most regulation has instead taken the form of commands and controls and that market incentive experiments are few suggests that the use of regulation as a tool of government policy cannot be ascribed to a widespread desire to perfect the workings of the private market.

Instead, the United States has relied on commands and controls, techniques designed to ensure that certain outcomes —a stable competitive environment or clean air and water —will be attained. To find a more adequate explanation of why regulatory measures in the U.S. have actually been adopted and pursued, political, and especially interest group, behavior must be examined.

Political Theories of Regulation
When faced with the critique of the market failure paradigm described above, regulatory theorists responded by analogizing regulatory efforts to expenditure programs; both, in this approach, are the products of political pressure brought to bear by important constituencies. Such positive models attempt to explain why the various market failures have not been automatically corrected by political action.

The positive view starts with the fact that we do not live in a frictionless democracy (the political analogue to a perfectly competitive market) where coalitions can be relied upon to ensure that market failures are corrected simply because, in principle, there may exist a set of corrective actions that will make everyone better off than they were before. Interest groups seek legislation because of the benefits such legislation will produce for *them;* they seek viable programs that will command majorities, not Pareto-superior outcomes that would assure unanimities. The positive approach to regulation places far more emphasis on the *distributional* effects of regulation than on its potential for enhancing economic efficiency.

The initial positive models of regulation were developed by Chicago economists primarily interested in explaining the rise of economic regulation. Although they rejected the market failure paradigm as an accurate predictor of actual regulatory outcomes, the Chicago economists borrowed from economic analysis the notion of self-interest to argue that regulation could be viewed as another traded commodity and therefore could be analyzed within the familiar economic framework of supply and demand.[4] Under this view, the votes and campaign support of elected officials merely replace dollars as the budget constraint. The demand for price and entry regulation, in this view, comes from firms in every industry and workers in every guild: such restrictive regulation simply raises the incomes or profits of existing firms and workers. Regulation is willingly supplied by elected officials who desire to finance and win elections. Price and entry regulation will result so long as no group with sufficient political and economic power enters to disrupt the market between the elected officials and their potential supporters by outbidding one group or the other.

This economic perspective of the politics of regulation draws support from the pre-1975 histories of several major economic regulatory programs. The railroad industry, for example, was placed under the regulatory eye of the Interstate Commerce Commission in 1887 more to guarantee service and subsidize travel to smaller cities and to prevent price wars than to address a market imperfection. Regulation of the trucking

4. The seminal work in this area is George Stigler, "The Theory of Economic Regulation," *The Bell Journal of Economics and Management Science,* Spring 1971, pp. 3–21. The theory has been formalized and refined in Richard Posner, "Theories of Economic Regulation," *Bell Journal of Economics,* Autumn 1974, pp. 335–58 and Sam Peltzman, "Toward a More General Theory of Regulation," *Journal of Law and Economics,* August 1976, pp. 211–40.

industry and intercity bus service came later, mainly because the rates of their principal competitor, the railroad industry, were already subject to regulation. Although passenger airline regulation was instituted to prevent the airlines from lowering passenger air fares in order to receive larger subsidy payments for airmail carriage, most airlines have fought to maintain price and entry regulation of their industry.[5]

There are numerous difficulties within the Chicago view, however. To begin with, it does not clearly explain why some interest groups succeed while others fail. Why can the truckers and shippers keep their regulations but not the airlines and banks? It is also difficult to reconcile the Chicago view with instances of price regulation. While agricultural producers have generally supported agricultural marketing orders, which tend to raise prices above free-market levels, the same can hardly be said for oil and gas producers, who have strongly opposed price controls, which have acted to depress prices below free-market levels.

A deeper problem arises in explaining the development of social regulation in terms of narrow economic self-interest. Given the clear power asymmetry between widely dispersed groups of citizens, on the one hand, and the concentrated economic power of business, on the other, how can the success of environmental and safety regulation affecting industries as powerful as the automobile and energy industries be explained? It seems clear that, if the economics of financing elections and the pattern of rents from regulatory programs alone determined the legislative outcomes, the major environmental, health, and safety statutes would never have been passed.[6]

Professor James Q. Wilson and his collaborators have provided a broader analytical framework applicable to social regulation that complements the Chicago theory. Under this view, both ideological and economic motivations can lead individuals and groups to seek regulatory intervention. In addition, this approach recognizes that legislative and regulatory decisions

5. *Economic Report of the President,* 1978, pp. 207–08.
6. See James Q. Wilson, *The Politics of Regulation* (New York: Basic Books, 1978), pp. 370–72.

can be strongly influenced by how widely and intensively the costs and benefits of the regulatory programs are distributed. Thus, unlike much economic regulation which, once in place, tends to be supported primarily by members of the regulated industries, social regulatory efforts generally have been backed by a significant majority of the public. Over 80 percent of the respondents to a 1983 Harris poll, for example, indicated that they wanted air pollution laws to be kept as tough as or more stringent than they are now.[7] Similarly, 59 percent in 1981 favored a strengthening of worker safety regulation.[8] Even discounting for the inherent fickleness of survey responses, it is generally agreed that environmental and safety regulation have broad public support.[9]

Wide public backing by itself, however, does not produce legislation. Entrepreneurs help form coalitions to raise public awareness and convince legislators either to enact or to retain regulatory legislation. In the case of economic regulation, the regulated firms have naturally performed that role. Their counterparts in the area of social regulation have been the civil rights and environmental groups, consumer organizations, and the labor unions.

It is possible, of course, to view each of the somewhat specialized interests that have supported social regulatory programs in strictly "economic" terms. For example, we indicated in the last chapter that although the benefits of social regulation, such as a cleaner and safer environment, are generally not traded in the marketplace, a dollar "price tag" can be assigned to these benefits *as if* they were so traded. In this view, the groups seeking a cleaner environment represent just as much an "economic" interest in environmental regulation as, say, trucking or airline companies represent in supporting price and entry regulation of their industries. A more direct economic interest lies behind civil rights or antidiscrimination regulations,

7. *Business Week;* January 24, 1983, p. 87.
8. *Public Opinion,* August/September 1981, p. 34.
9. See Everett C. Ladd, "Clearing the Air: Opinion and Public Policy on the Environment," *Public Opinion,* February/March 1982, p. 16.

which affect the economic welfare of varous minority groups, an expressly "economic" objective. Similarly, the economic stakes are clear for worker safety regulation, which not surprisingly has been pressed by labor unions on behalf of their employee-members. What can be gained through regulation need not be negotiated for at the bargaining table.

Such an approach stretches the analysis pretty thin. The case for social regulation in many situations has been pressed primarily from ideological conviction—that a clean and safe environment, a safe workplace, and a society where equal opportunity is ensured are important for their own sake.[10] These convictions have, from time to time, been fueled by a wider public outrage at social injustices. Thus, meat inspection legislation was passed at the turn of the twentieth century in response to public concern following Upton Sinclair's powerful indictment of the unhealthy practices in the meat industry. Public horror after the thalidomide deaths provided much of the impetus for the reforms in drug regulation. And environmental legislation passed in the late 1960s and early 1970s responded to a widespread public concern that dirty air and water posed a threat to human health and diminished the nation's quality of life. As we discuss in greater detail in the next chapter, these strong convictions in some cases led to the enactment of absolutist regulatory statutes that precluded regulatory agencies from balancing costs against benefits in making regulatory decisions.

The ideological fervor of the interest groups that have supported social regulation, coupled with widespread public support, has helped to produce the recent explosion in such regulation. Although social regulatory programs date from the early 1900s, virtually all of the major regulatory statutes passed between 1962 and 1978 fall into the category of social regulation—from the Food and Drug Amendments of 1962 requiring the pretesting of drugs for efficacy (in addition to the

---

10. In the language of Arthur Okun, such values can be said to lie outside the "domain of dollars." Arthur M. Okun, *Equality and Efficiency: The Big Tradeoff* (Washington, D.C.: The Brookings Institution, 1976).

earlier requirements of safety), to the 1966 National Motor Vehicle Traffic Safety Act authorizing the promulgation of mandatory automobile safety standards, to the Clean Air Act of 1970, and to the 1976 Toxic Substances Control Act requiring advance testing and restrictions on the use of chemical substances. In all, over forty major pieces of legislation dealing with social regulation were passed during this sixteen-year period.[11] The sheer scale and timing of this legislative effort suggest that Congress has been concerned with more than just correcting a series of run-of-the-mill market failures.

In sum, regulation is as subject to the ebb and flow of broad political forces as it is to the variable powers of parochial interests of specific groups that feel the effects of regulatory activities most intensely and directly. It should not be surprising, therefore, that the political solutions have produced outcomes as imperfect as the unregulated market itself.

How We Regulate

As we have just indicated, a necessary but not sufficient condition for the implementation of a regulatory program is that there exist a strong political demand for that program. Generally, that demand is pressed most vigorously by particular groups that stand to reap the greatest benefit from the institution of the specific initiative, although, as we have also suggested, the success of those groups will hinge in considerable part on the prevailing political climate.

The pressures of the various interest groups to adopt particular regulatory programs, in turn, have appeared in two central features of how the nation has proceeded with its regulatory activity.

First, as each regulatory initiative has been adopted, Congress has generally created a new agency to carry it out rather than entrusted its implementation to an existing body. As a result, numerous single mission agencies now dot the Washing-

11. Murray L. Weidenbaum, *Business, Government, and the Public*, 2nd ed. (Englewood Cliffs, N.J.: Prentice Hall, 1981), pp. 7–11.

ton environs, classified along industry lines for economic regulatory initiatives (airlines, communications, surface transportation) and along functional lines for social regulatory programs (consumer safety, environmental, food and drug, and occupational safety). Of particular importance is that no branch of the federal government has been given overall responsibility for all regulatory decisions, since only some agencies have been lodged in the executive branch, while others have been made independent of both the executive and the Congress.

This fractionalization of regulatory responsibilities has been exacerbated by a second noteworthy feature of the current regulatory process: the nature of the rulemaking process itself. The regulations that administrative agencies issue are generally developed and judged on their own particular merits. Rarely do agencies compare the costs and benefits of their various rules or compare them against the rules developed and promulgated by other agencies. This is not an accident, for the authorizing legislation sets quite different standards for different agencies. The individualized nature of the rulemaking process is reinforced by the trial-like procedures that govern agency rulemakings to ensure that due process of law is afforded to interested parties and by the prospect of judicial review of the rules that are finally promulgated.[12]

In short, the nation pursues its multiple regulatory objectives in a highly fragmented and decentralized fashion. Decentralization is a virtue in a market economy, because the market mechanism harmonizes the competing claims advanced by firms and consumers on society's limited pool of available resources. There is no invisible hand to coordinate activities in the public sector, however; resources will not be allocated efficiently in the absence of some type of decision-making apparatus to perform the role that the market assumes in the private sector.

1. The Proliferation of Single Mission Agencies
The nation has come a long way since its first regulatory

12. See Lester B. Lave, "Conflicting Objectives in Regulating Automobiles," *Science* May 22, 1981, pp. 893–99.

agency, the Steamboat Inspection Service, was established in 1837. By the turn of the century, the number of regulatory agencies had grown to five; on the eve of the New Deal, the number stood at just short of fifteen; and today, depending on how they are counted, the number of regulatory agencies stands at over eighty.

Despite the explosion in their number, the regulatory agencies all along have been recognized as peculiar institutions. Because the Founding Fathers did not have to consider the need for an Interstate Commerce Commission, an Environmental Protection Agency, or a Nuclear Regulatory Commission, they never had to decide at what point on the scale of checks and balances these agencies should be placed. The Constitution and Federalist Papers are understandably silent both on *how* to delegate the diverse (quasi-legislative, quasi-executive, and quasi-judicial) regulatory powers and *how much* power to transfer to these bodies.

Congress has resolved these questions by creating two kinds of regulatory agencies: executive branch and independent. An agency is said to belong to the executive branch if its members serve at the pleasure of the President. The independent agencies have members who are generally appointed by the President and confirmed by the Senate and can generally be removed only with "cause."

The major regulatory agencies, classified by type, are listed in table 3.2. Although the table reflects our stark division between the executive and independent branches, there is in fact a continuum of independence in the way these agencies actually operate. At one extreme, for example, is the fiercely independent Federal Reserve Board. Although sometimes said to be a creature of Congress under the "to coin money" clause of the Constitution, the Federal Reserve exercises its money market functions independently of either Congress or the President. At the other extreme, perhaps, is the Commodity Credit Corporation, which simply ratifies presidential or Agriculture Department directives.[13]

---

13. Despite these distinctions between the independent and executive branch agencies, which admittedly are overly neat, there are certain anomalies.

Table 3.2. Twenty Important Federal Regulatory Agencies[a]

Independent	Executive Branch (Dependent)
Federal Reserve Board	Environmental Protection
Federal Energy Regulatory	Agency
Commission	Occupational Safety and
Federal Communications	Health Administration
Commission	Food and Drug Administration
Federal Trade Commission	Office of Surface Mining
Nuclear Regulatory Commission	Comptroller of the Currency
Securities Exchange Commission	National Transportation
International Trade Commission	Safety Administration
Consumer Product Safety	National Highway Traffic
Commission	Safety Administration
National Labor Relations Board	Economic Regulatory
Interstate Commerce Commission	Administration
Federal Maritime Commission	
Civil Aeronautics Board	

[a]The agencies identified above were listed as the eighteen key Federal agencies engaged in "economic, safety, and health regulation" by the *Study on Federal Regulation,* Committee on Government Operations, United States Senate, February 1977, volume 2, p. 2. We have modified that list by folding the Federal Energy Administration and Federal Power Commission into the Economic Regulatory Administration of the Department of Energy and the Federal Energy Regulatory Commission. We have further added the recently created Office of Surface Mining (in the Department of the Interior) and the International Trade Commission for a grand total of twenty "important" regulatory agencies, of which twelve are independent and eight are lodged in the executive branch.

Two contrasting problems have arisen as the agencies in each of these branches have been created: (1) the number of agency employees with narrow perspectives has proliferated, but (2) none has been charged with coordinating the regulatory effort as a whole and attempting to balance competing national

For example, the independent Consumer Product Safety Commission undertakes tasks that are similar to those of other social regulatory agencies lodged within the executive branch. The central policy-making body of the Federal Reserve System (the Federal Open Market Committee) is unique in that five of its members are elected by the private sector. Imagine the uproar if almost half of the ICC were elected by truckers.

objectives. Of course, regulatory agencies have no monopoly on tunnel vision. It is unusual in policy debates, for example, to find the Agriculture Department allowing inflationary impacts to impede price support programs or the Defense Department slowing deployment of certain weapons systems because of their potential environmental impacts. Yet, as we will emphasize in the following chapter, the nation has established a centralized method of considering and trading off such competing objectives through the federal expenditure budget process. No analogous process yet exists for regulation.

At the simplest level, the proliferation and overlap of regulatory agencies are routinely blamed for some of the regulatory horrors that are often produced to show what a mess the system is in. For example, a meat packing company was told by one federal agency to wash its floors several times a day for cleanliness and by another to keep its floor at all times dry to prevent employee accidents. The steel industry has to comply with over 5,000 regulations, administered by twenty-five federal agencies and numerous state and local agencies. There are cases in which firms have been told by the EPA to keep harmful emissions inside their plants lest they damage the outside environment and at the same time have been told by OSHA to vent emissions outside their plants lest the workers inside be injured.[14]

A recent and more serious example of regulatory overlap lies in the administration of cancer policy. At least five Federal agencies (EPA, CPSC, OSHA, FDA, USDA) have the authority to regulate carcinogenic substances. Prior to 1979, they were unable to agree on the scientific principles to be used to determine when a substance could even be classified as carcinogenic. Even though these differences have now been partially resolved, the regulatory approaches of the five agencies still vary considerably.[15]

14. For a summary of many of the problems plaguing the regulatory process and an outline of solutions offered during the Carter administration, see Richard Neustadt, *Regulatory Reform: President Carter's Program* (Washington, D.C.: White House Domestic Policy Office, 1980).

15. For a discussion of the Regulatory Council's efforts to harmonize OSHA's cancer policies with the cancer policies of other federal regulatory agencies, see note 26 in chapter 4, below.

Similarly, overlap occurs when various agencies impose widely different regulations on the same industry and firms within that industry. For example, many manufacturing industries in the United States—autos, steel, and chemicals—are affected by the regulations of numerous agencies: environmental regulations of the EPA, worker safety regulations of OSHA, employment discrimination regulations of the Labor Department and the EEOC, and trade regulations of the FTC, to name just a few. Is any individual or agency charged with adding up the total cost imposed by all these regulations combined? In particular, is any effort made to coordinate the various rules to ensure that only those with the highest priority are imposed first?

As we indicate in the following chapter, the Regulatory Council under the Carter administration made attempts to fulfill these functions but, by design, was capable of achieving only limited success. The Reagan administration has been sensitive to the cumulative impact of federal regulation on the auto industry, in particular, but has abolished the Regulatory Council and has undertaken no real effort to rationalize the regulation of other industries. In short, there exists today no mechanism or procedure that requires the systematic consideration of the cumulative impact of regulatory burdens on particular industries, how these impacts can be moderated without sacrificing progress toward worthwhile regulatory objectives, or how the objectives themselves can be balanced against each other.

The proliferation and overlap of regulatory agencies and responsibilities would be of little concern if someone with line authority were in a position to take responsibility for adjudicating disputes or assuring that regulatory decisions as a whole are balanced. Yet it is precisely because the number of agencies has proliferated that the lines of authority are unclear. Who carries the ultimate legal responsibility for all regulatory decisions? How "independent" are regulatory agencies? To what extent can the President (or Congress) direct the activities of the various regulatory agencies?

In the case of the independent agencies, there is little question that the Congress has created a series of mini-governments that (except for the FTC, which has collided with Congress in recent years) operate virtually autonomously. As was noted by the Brownlow Commission in 1937:[16]

[Independent commissions] are in reality miniature independent governments set up to deal with the railroad problem, the banking problem, or the radio problem. They constitute a headless "fourth branch" of the government, a haphazard deposit of irresponsible agencies and uncoordinated powers. They do violence to the basic theory of the American Constitution that there should be three branches of government and only three.

More recently a similar view of the executive branch agencies has been described by the former counsel to President Carter, Lloyd Cutler:[17]

Every school child learns about the separation of powers. The Federal Government has three branches—legislative, executive, judicial. Right? Wrong.

Oh, yes, we forgot the regulatory branch. The ICC, the CAB, the FCC, the SEC, the FTC, the NLRB, the FEC, the CPSC, and about a dozen other agencies operate under laws that make them independent of the legislative and executive branches. So there are really four branches. Right? Wrong, because each of these independent agencies is also independent of every other agency. So that makes about 23 branches? Careful, you may be wrong again.

For there is a new theory abroad in the land that even regulatory agencies *within* the executive branch are also independent of the President and of one another. There are over 60 such agencies, many of them parts of a cabinet department.

---

16. The President's Committee on Administrative Management, "Report of the Committee with Studies of Administrative Management in the Federal Government," as printed in Subcommittee on Separation of Powers, Committee on the Judiciary, U.S. Senate, *Separation of Powers and the Independent Agencies: Cases and Selected Readings,* 91st Congress, 1st Session, pp. 345–46, 1969.

17. Lloyd N. Cutler, "Who Masters the Regulators?" *Washington Post,* October 17, 1978.

The view to which Cutler referred is the recent claim by the new Jeffersonians—led by certain environmental and public interest groups—that the executive branch agencies, too, effectively constitute separate branches of government outside of direct presidential control. Under this view, when Congress directs the Secretary of Labor to set worker safety standards under the OSH Act, the Administrator of the EPA to set environmental regulations, and the Secretary of Transportation to establish automobile safety regulations, Congress means that *only these officials*—and not the President—are to make the final regulatory decisions. Presidential involvement in the rulemaking decisions of these agencies is therefore taken to represent a circumvention of express congressional directives and a violation of the rulemaking procedures established by the Administrative Procedure Act (discussed below).

Contemporary Federalists take an entirely different approach. Under this view, the President runs or should run the executive branch. By virtue of his constitutional power to "hire and fire" subordinate employees and his constitutional responsibility to "see that the laws are faithfully executed," the President has the final word on all decisions authorized to be made by executive officials.

During the Carter administration, several skirmishes between these opposing forces ended in court. In the cotton dust episode discussed below, it appeared at one time that the final regulations issued by OSHA might be attacked because of "improper" presidential involvement. Later, the Council of Economic Advisers was sued by an environmental consortium attempting (ultimately without success) to restrain it from discussing the 1978 surface mining regulation with the Interior Department. Similar concerns were raised in the legal challenge to the EPA's regulations related to ozone and the new source performance standards for steam-electric utility generating plants (the so-called sulfur scrubbing rule).

Thus far, the courts have come down squarely on the side of the federalists.[18] In addition, the Reagan administration has

18. See the discussion of the *Sierra Club v. Costle* decision in chapter 5.

followed that view in centralizing regulatory oversight over the individual rules of the executive branch agencies, as we discuss in the following chapter. Most recently, in early 1983 President Reagan felt compelled to accept a change of leadership at EPA, to register a symbolic and, probably, a significant reorientation of the agency's policy direction. Such prompt and dramatic changes would not have been possible had the EPA been established as an independent agency. There is little question that the federalist view is an important ingredient in effective regulatory management. If the Jeffersonian thesis of independence were upheld by the courts, it would be a major step *backward* in the control of the regulatory process by elected officials.

Yet even under the federalist view, which accords to the President the authority to direct, to a large extent, the regulatory activities of the agencies within the executive branch, the lines of authority over the rulemaking process remain, in practice, less than clear. First, the President has no legal authority under any circumstances to control the activities of the independent agencies. Second, and perhaps more important, presidential or centralized Executive Office review and control of *individual* rulemaking decisions is far different in character from such centralized coordination of regulatory priorities within and across agencies. As we discuss in succeeding chapters, while some progress has been achieved during the two most recent administrations in achieving some control of the first type, no mechanism is in place that establishes the latter.

In arguing that the current regulatory system is excessively fragmented and disorganized, we are of course aware that these features are not unknown in other arenas. Indeed, given the cost of information gathering and decision-making and the scarcity of time of top decision-makers, a fair amount of muddling through and incremental decision-making is sensible. But to say that information about regulation is costly does not mean that it should not be gathered at all. To say we cannot continuously make broad national decisions on the share of GNP to be devoted to meeting regulatory objectives does not imply that the issue should never be addressed. And to say that Congress's time is scarce does not imply that congressmen should ignore broad issues of regulatory policy. In short, the degree of regulatory muddle and fragmentation seems far beyond the bounds of reason.

2. The Rulemaking Process

The fragmentation of the nation's regulatory effort is furthered by basic features of the way in which regulations are actually developed. Although regulations clearly resemble legislation, since a regulation fills in a blank left open by an authorizing statute, the *process* of setting regulations resembles, to varying degrees, a judicial proceeding in which specific facts are found, precedents followed, and requirements of rationality imposed.[19] Each of these features—substantive and procedural—contains attributes that contribute to the dispersion of responsibility for regulatory decisions.

Regulators fill in the blanks because Congress delegates regulatory functions to the agencies. Each agency, in turn, is generally charged with implementing numerous statutes, each of which may contain multiple instructions to establish various rules. For example, the EPA is responsible for setting regulations under the Clean Air Act, the Federal Water Pollution Control Act, and the Toxic Substances Control Act, to name just a few. The Clean Air Act alone contains numerous standard-setting provisions, such as directives to set ambient air quality standards for certain established pollutants (e.g., carbon monoxide, sulfur dioxide, nitrogen oxide, ozone) and emissions standards for new stationary and mobile sources.

Faced with these multiple responsibilities, how do the agencies proceed? Do they fill in many blanks at the same time by drafting their regulations broadly to cover a wide class of situations, or are rules developed incrementally and somewhat narrowly? For example, does the EPA set ambient standards for all "criteria" pollutants at once, or are each of the standards set in separate rulemakings? From the vantage of interest and

19. As Judge Mikva has stated: "an agency is not a legislature." *State Farm v. NHTSA*, 680 F.2d. 206, 221 (D.C. Cir. 1982).

constituency groups, the narrow approach is far preferable, because strong (or weak) agency action is easier to obtain on an isolated set of problems than it is when a wide variety of problems, and therefore interests, are lumped together in a single package. In the latter case, there are generally more opportunities for trading off interests and objectives than in the case where the rule itself is very narrow and addresses an isolated set of objectives.

With very few exceptions, agencies in fact regulate narrowly and incrementally, addressing a single problem or hazard a step at a time. Moreover, the rulemakings themselves tend to channel attention solely toward the questions directly related to that issue and away from other relevant, but less directly related, information. For example, when OSHA sets a standard governing worker exposure to arsenic, it does not take into account the comparative costs and benefits of regulating worker exposure to other toxic substances. Similarly, when EPA sets its ambient air quality standard for carbon monoxide, it does not consider whether a more cost-effective method of cleaning the air could be attained by trading off the stringency of that particular standard against the stringency of its ambient standards for such other pollutants as sulfur dioxide and nitrogen dioxide. Such tunnel vision leads to a highly inefficient cumulative result, because no tradeoffs between regulations are allowed.

It is instructive to review how the exercise of delegated regulatory authority in even a relatively narrow area can have unforeseen private sector effects. During the Carter administration, the Department of Transportation issued a regulation to help provide access for the handicapped to mass-transit systems. The regulation, which, as we note in chapter 5, was subsequently rescinded by the Reagan administration, had its origins in a one-liner in the Rehabilitation Act of 1973, which stated that

> no otherwise qualified handicapped individual in the United States
> . . . shall, solely by reason of his handicap, be excluded from
> participation in, be denied the benefits of, or be subjected to

discrimination under any program or activity receiving Federal financial assistance (29 U.S.C. §790).

The content of the statutory sentence was progressively filled out by administrative interpretations to the point where the final regulation required the retrofitting of a large number of subway stations throughout the U.S. to provide elevator access for persons in wheelchairs, at a total cost estimated in the billions of dollars, and at costs per ride estimated in excess of $5.

Where did the authority come from? Certainly not from the sentence just cited nor from the legislative history. One committee member, Representative Charles Vanik, observed that, in drafting the legislation, Congress had no idea that subways would be included.[20] Even though most of the subway funds would be provided by as yet unappropriated federal outlays, no conscious congressional decision to allocate these funds was actually made. Nor was there any visible sign that the President knew of the costs and benefits of the original proposal. In short, Congress unwittingly wrote a blank check to "aid the handicapped." The regulators simply filled in the blanks.[21]

We do not quarrel here with the objective of the 1973 Rehabilitation Act, which provided the statutory authority for DOT's regulation. The point is rather that the equal access rule was developed in total isolation from other important objectives—to the handicapped, to transportation generally, and to the nation as a whole. For example, no one addressed during the course of the equal access rulemaking the question of

20. See Timothy B. Clark, "Access for the Handicapped—A Test of Carter's War on Inflation," *National Journal,* October 21, 1978, p. 1672.

21. The U.S. Court of Appeals for the Second Circuit has recently made clear that the 1973 Rehabilitation Act also requires mass transit agencies at the local level to take at least "modest, affirmative steps" to accommodate the handicapped in public transporation. The court reinstated a suit that had been dismissed by the District Court below on the ground that the act does not require "massive expenditures" to make all transportation systems accessible to wheelchair users; the Second Circuit held that the District Court below should have considered less costly alternatives, such as separate services for the handicapped. See Dopico v. Goldschmidt, 687 F2d 644 (2d. Cir. 1982).

whether a *package* of services to the handicapped population generally—including some transportation services—could be designed that would deliver a more valuable range of services at lower costs. Similarly, neither DOT nor Congress explicitly addressed the question of how much of the nation's limited resources should be spent on, say, retrofitting subways for the handicapped versus other national objectives, such as cleaning the air or water, filling potholes, or preventing subway crime. Such larger issues necessarily get lost in the course of narrow agency rulemaking.

The isolated nature of regulatory decision-making is reinforced by the quasi-judicial aspect of the procedures that govern individual rulemakings. By their very nature, judicial proceedings are far more narrowly focused than legislative or policy deliberations. A trial, for example, is governed by strict rules of evidence and by certain legal standards that narrow the range of outcomes. Rulemakings are more flexible but still must abide by both the substantive standards set in regulatory statutes and by certain procedural guidelines.

The process by which federal regulations are issued is governed by the Administrative Procedure Act (APA), under which regulations are broadly developed through one of two procedural models: *formal* or *informal* procedures. Formal rulemakings are closely analogous to judicial proceedings, since they are governed by rules of evidence and generally employ live testimony under oath and cross-examination. Such procedures are typically used in situations that call for judicial resolution: where the number of parties is small and the issues are primarily factual, such as the granting of a license or franchise. The functions of the economic regulatory agencies—the CAB, FCC, ICC, for example—fall primarily into this category, because their rules are primarily adjudicatory in nature: the awarding of air routes, trucking certificates, and broadcasting licenses, inspection and issuance of permits for nuclear reactors, and the determination of injury from foreign competition. These are generally narrow functions that often involve the purely distributional issues raised in assigning valuable property rights and are therefore well-suited for resolution through the use of quasi-adjudicatory techniques. Informal rulemakings, on the other hand, are more legislative in character. Under informal procedures, an agency need only issue a notice announcing the initiation of a rulemaking and soliciting public comments. When it issues its final rule, the agency must provide, in a "Statement of Basis and Purpose," the factual and logical bases for its decision as well as a reasoned analysis of how it reached its conclusions.[22] The social regulatory agencies largely use informal rulemaking procedures. Since social regulatory issues tend to affect large numbers of individuals and firms and to raise as many, if not more, policy questions than factual issues, formal procedures would be highly unwieldy. The flexibility of informal procedures makes them far better suited, therefore, to developing responses to the problems addressed by social regulatory programs.

Interested parties have the opportunity to seek review of agency decisions in the federal courts.[23] As a general rule, the standard of review is somewhat tougher in the case of formal rulemakings than for informal rulemakings, as one would expect from the stronger judicial character of formal proceedings. Thus, a rule developed through formal rulemaking will be struck down by a court if it is found to be unsupported by "substantial evidence" in the rulemaking record or otherwise in violation of the agency's statutory mandate. A rule developed through informal procedures, however, can be struck only if it is found to be either "arbitrary and capricious" (a looser standard than "substantial evidence") or not in accord with the relevant authorizing statute.

Most important federal regulation today is developed through procedures that tend to be closer to the informal than

22. Over time, the distinction between formal and informal procedures has been blurred somewhat by the tendency of both Congress and the agencies to add certain "formal" procedures—such as hearings, rebuttal opportunities, and in some cases, limited cross-examination—to the bare-minimum requirements for informal rulemaking.

23. Many statutes provide for review to be taken directly to the Courts of Appeals, bypassing the lower District Courts.

the formal rulemaking model. Correspondingly, the regulatory issues we examine in this book tend to arise far more frequently in the context of informal rather than formal rulemakings. The point that bears emphasis is that even when rules are developed using informal procedures, the rulemaking process contributes to the fragmentation of regulatory decisions. Such rules are subject to review in court for both substantive and procedural propriety. The quasi-judicial atmosphere surrounding the development of all regulation stifles the comparison and trading off of multiple regulatory objectives within and across agencies. The focus instead is defensive rather than creative, concerned primarily with the validity of the individual rule at hand and on whether it passes muster, under applicable legal standards, on its own particular merits.

In sum, the regulatory process we have described in this chapter is the outgrowth of a political process that has shaped both the substance of the problems tackled and the manner in which they are addressed. The feature that stands out is that regulatory issues are typically confronted individually and incrementally. Responsibility for regulatory decisions is diffused throughout numerous agencies in multiple separate branches of government. And no one branch or process exists to require elected officials in both political branches—the Congress and the Executive—to step back, look at the regulatory effort as a whole, and set priorities for what should be accomplished and in what order.

It is with this understanding that we proceed to examine systematically what is wrong with the current regulatory process and how to correct the problems that exist.

4

The Political and Economic
Defects of the Regulatory Process

In the last two chapters, we have outlined the organizing principles, as well as the economic impacts, of the current federal regulatory system. Now we turn to the central issue—whether the system is working well.

As we suggested in chapter 1, government regulation has often been criticized for imposing either too much red tape or too heavy a cost burden on the private sector. Relatively little attention, however, has been given to the systemic flaws in the process—the insufficient degree of political accountability for regulatory decisions and the inefficient method by which the nation has thus far attempted to accomplish its regulatory objectives.

In this chapter, we examine these institutional defects on two levels. First, we address the *political defects* of the current system by examining the inadequacy of current oversight efforts by both political branches—the Congress and the Executive. Then we turn to the *inefficiency* plaguing the current effort, which we believe can be traced not only to the absence of effective oversight that would constrain regulators to allocate resources efficiently, but to undesirable statutory restrictions inhibiting agencies from balancing costs against benefits and from choosing less costly marketlike incentives instead of rigid command-and-control regulatory techniques.

Inadequate Political Oversight

There is a need in any organization or society for an oversight mechanism, that is, a process of higher-level review of the decisions made by individuals and institutions at lower levels. For regulatory decisions, oversight could occur at three levels at which either or both the Congress and the Executive are involved, as illustrated in figure 4.1. The narrowest level—the review of individual rules—is represented by the inner rectangle. Such review could occur either as the rules are developed or, as in the case of judicial review, after they have been

Figure 4.1. Levels of Oversight of Regulatory Decisions

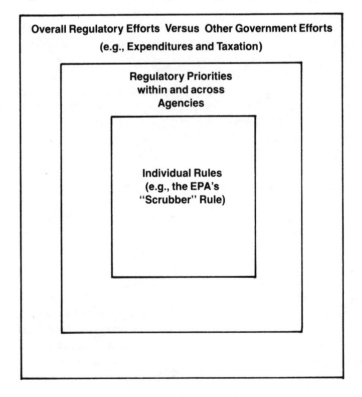

Overall Regulatory Efforts Versus Other Government Efforts (e.g., Expenditures and Taxation)

Regulatory Priorities within and across Agencies

Individual Rules (e.g., the EPA's "Scrubber" Rule)

promulgated. The second tier of oversight relates to the setting of priorities among different regulatory programs, both within agencies—such as the air, water, and hazardous waste regulatory programs administered by the EPA—and across agencies (EPA, OSHA, FTC, etc.). This second type of review could occur, at least in part, before individual regulatory proposals are actually formulated. The highest level of review (the largest rectangle) involves the comparison of the total impact of regulation—in terms of both costs and benefits—with that of other government efforts, such as expenditures and taxation. At this level of aggregation, the priority-setting decision—whether to spend directly through government expenditures or indirectly through regulation—is analogous to the "guns vs. butter" allocation that political decision-makers now routinely confront in deciding upon the level of federal expenditures.

As we discuss further below, regulatory oversight has largely been confined to the first of these levels—the review of individual regulations—and has been exercised primarily by the executive branch.[1] In addition, executive oversight itself has been limited by various statutory restrictions on the balancing of costs and benefits (discussed later in this chapter), which sharply limit the agencies' abilities to choose among various regulatory options and, correspondingly, the efforts of others to oversee or direct those choices.[2]

1. As we indicate in the following chapters, Congress has granted itself the authority to veto individual regulations promulgated under various statutes. This authority has rarely been used and is subject to strong constitutional challenge.

2. Oversight at the two higher levels—which is centered on the regulatory *agendas* of the agencies rather than on the specific rules they issue—is, in one sense, less hampered by statutory criteria. Thus, under both the Clean Air Act and the Federal Water Pollution Control Act and related amendments, the EPA sets ambient standards for whatever pollutants it may identify (although once it has identified such pollutants, the EPA has much less discretion in setting technology-based effluent or emission standards). The CPSC and OSHA are given even broader mandates. Both are simply charged with the responsibility for regulating "harmful substances," as determined by the agency. Similarly, the NHTSA is directed by the Motor Vehicle Safety Act to set auto safety standards that are "reasonable" and "practicable." *(Continued next page.)*

It can be argued, of course, that Congress has available to it a variety of instruments, including approval authority over agency appointees and appropriations, through which it can also exercise oversight functions. These instruments, however, have generally not been used effectively as oversight tools. Moreover, none is currently designed to permit Congress (and the Executive) to perform effective oversight at the higher two levels, relating to the determination of priorities between various regulatory programs and to the overall impact of all regulatory decisions.

1. Congressional Oversight
Congress can oversee and exercise control over the regulatory process by controlling four important functions: appointments, authorization, appropriations, and substantive review. Congressional oversight in the first three of these areas was reviewed in 1977 by the Senate Government Operations Committee in its *Study on Federal Regulation.*[3] Although the methodology of that study does not permit precise conclusions, its thoroughness is impressive, and we draw on its findings below.

The first technique that can be used to influence the direction of policy is the appointments process. Although the Senate must approve senior agency appointees, the appointment of regulatory officials in practice has clearly been an executive branch prerogative. Below Cabinet levels (that is, for virtually

---

The ability of some agencies to set their agendas is limited, however, by statutory deadlines. For example, the EPA must abide by statutory timetables in setting water pollution standards and for approving State Implementation Plans (SIPs) for controlling air pollution.

To the extent discretion may be exercised, the setting of the regulatory agenda becomes one of the most important, and often overlooked, functions that agencies perform, since the setting of regulatory priorities can have as much economic impact as the decision of how to regulate in any given case.

3. Committee on Government Operations, United States Senate, *Study on Federal Regulation.* Volume 1 of the study is entitled "The Regulatory Appointments Process" and dated January 1977. Volume 2 is entitled "Congressional Oversight of Regulatory Agencies," and dated February 1977.

all regulatory appointments except the most important ones like the chairman of the Board of Governors of the Federal Reserve) little care is generally taken to assure that the appointees are of high quality or have acceptable political views. One clearly documented example is that of the ICC commissioners, for whom the average duration of confirmation hearings over several decades was seventeen minutes.[4] The *Study on Federal Regulation* reported that as of 1977 some progress had been made in improving congressional attention to the confirmation process.[5] Nevertheless, even with closer scrutiny of regulatory officials prior to their appointment, the Senate can at best have only extremely limited influence on how regulatory policy will be implemented thereafter.

The second technique of congressional oversight relating to the legislative process offers a substantial potential for congressional control because it is through authorization that Congress exercises life and death authority over government agencies. Moreover, it is at the authorization stage that Congress designs the goals, processes, and techniques of regulation.

In practice, however, congressional control over agency authorizations is flawed in three significant respects. As we highlight later in this chapter, the statutory goals of regulatory agencies are often so broad and/or vague as to provide little meaningful guidance either to the agencies or to Congress in reviewing agency actions. This problem is aggravated by authorized regulatory techniques that are generally poorly designed. Finally, and for present purposes most importantly, some statutes confer perpetual authorization, and those that are temporary are rarely seriously reexamined.

Table 4.1 gives a partial list of the authorization periods of some major regulatory agencies. The table clearly indicates that many of these agencies are either given permanent authorizations (implying no periodic review) or are not authorized at all. The statutory charters of some agencies, of course, are changed

4. *Study on Federal Regulation,* vol. 2, p. 60.
5. *Study on Federal Regulation,* vol. 2., p. 62.

Table 4.1. Authorization Periods of Major Regulatory
            Agencies

Permanent Authorization	Periodic Authorization (in years)	No Authorization
CAB[a]	CFTC (4)	FDA
EPA	CPSC (4)	FMC
FCC	FTC (3)	Federal Reserve Board
ICC	NHTSA (2)	
NLRB	NTSB (2)	
OSHA	SEC (2)	
	NRC (1)	

SOURCE: *Study on Federal Regulation,* vol. 2, p. 46.
ᵃAuthorization for CAB was permanent until the Airline Deregulation Act of 1978 scheduled the agency for abolition in 1985.

from time to time. Of the fifteen agencies in table 4.1, two (the CAB and the FPC) were completely overhauled in the 1977–82 period, while the mandates of four others (the EPA, the ICC, the FTC, and the FRB) have been subject to significant changes.[6] The other agencies, however, have been relatively untouched by legislative overview in the last six years, during which legislative activity by historical standards was heavy.

The third oversight technique is the appropriations power, the most jealously guarded of all congressional powers. In theory, congressional authority over appropriations offers an attractive route through which Congress can regularly monitor and direct the regulatory activities of administrative agencies.[7] Nevertheless, this tool too has drawbacks as a method of effective political oversight of regulatory decision-making.

6. The *Study on Federal Regulation,* vol. 2, p. 48, reports that although, as of 1977, the statutory mandates of the ICC, CAB, and FCC had been amended nearly seventy times, the amendments were generally not intended "to direct and control" the policies of the agencies, and thus "were not used for control or oversight purposes."

7. The *Study on Federal Regulation,* vol. 2, p. 33, states: "Appropriations oversight is the most potent form of congressional oversight."

First, Congress has historically paid little attention to the operating budgets of the regulatory agencies. For example, in 1977 the Agriculture Department received 1,707 pages of direct testimony regarding its appropriation. Among regulatory agencies, however, the Federal Power Commission received seventy-seven pages, the Federal Communications Commission seventy-three, and the Civil Aeronautics Board ninety-three. Moreover, each regulatory agency figure was down substantially from the number of pages recorded in 1971.[8]

Similarly, the appropriations committees generally have had little effect on the regulatory process through the non-statutory recommendations (those not having force of law) often made in legislative reports or appropriations. For example, of thirty-two identified nonstatutory directives made by appropriations committees for fiscal year 1977, only two could be identified as an involvement in regulatory policy.[9] Our view, both from this data and from personal experience, is that non-statutory recommendations have had negligible weight in regulatory decision-making.

More fundamentally, the appropriations process is likely to be an ineffective means of monitoring and controlling the social cost of regulation because the lion's share of costs imposed by regulation is off-budget and borne by the private sector. The goal of the appropriations committees is to protect the Treasury; reducing mandated private outlays will not show up in a reduced budget deficit. Similarly, although reductions in agency operating budgets may translate into reductions in costs incurred by the private sector, they do so in a highly haphazard and undiscriminating fashion. In short, control over agency operating budgets is not an adequate substitute for overseeing

8. The pages of direct testimony are a rough index of the time actually spent in committee hearings. These data are from *Study on Federal Regulation,* vol. 2, p. 22.

9. *Study on Federal Regulation,* vol. 2, pp. 37–39. The two substantive recommendations were (1) that the CPSC establish a list of priorities in its prevention programs and (2) that OSHA not delay standards just in order to conduct studies. The extent to which these directives were even listened to is not clear.

and controlling the manner in which *private* resources are allocated through regulation to meet *government*-mandated policy objectives.

The final method of oversight available to Congress is the review of specific major regulations. Here too, congressional oversight comes up short. Congressional involvement in matters raised in individual rulemakings has been relatively infrequent; the notable recent exceptions include the 1974 congressional ban on the ignition interlock seat belt and the frequent congressional consideration of legislative vetoes of rules promulgated by the FTC.[10] Beyond these instances of congressional involvement, however, there are fundamental political and constitutional reasons, which we discuss further in the following chapter, why any such involvement in specific rulemakings is incapable of providing the type of systematic review of regulatory decision-making that is necessary and appropriate.

In sum, congressional oversight of the regulatory process is generally weak and highly sporadic. The control that has been exercised has focused on features of the process—appointees, agency authorizations, and annual agency operating budgets—that are at best distantly related to the private-sector impacts of regulation. More specifically, none of the existing congressional oversight mechanisms has permitted Congress to set priorities among diverse regulatory programs effectively and to control the total private-sector impact of all federal regulatory activity.

10. Barry Weingast and Mark Moran have recently offered a persuasive demonstration that the FTC has responded effectively to the views of that agency's congressional oversight committees. *See* Barry R. Weingast and Mark J. Moran, "The Myth of the Runaway Bureaucracy: The Case of the FTC." *Regulation,* May/June 1982, pp. 33–38. However, even this evidence establishes only that congressional influence has affected agency actions at the broadest level—namely, the degree to which the agency has pursued an "activist" policy in its rulemaking and enforcement activities—and has not proceeded from a careful consideration of the costs and benefits of individual FTC initiatives. Moreover, the continuous congressional attention given to the activities of the FTC is unique and has not been replicated with respect to other agencies.

2. *Executive Oversight*

In contrast with the relatively ineffective oversight efforts of the legislative branch, the executive has recently made considerable progress, particularly during the Carter and Reagan administrations, in establishing its own oversight procedures. Various agencies within the Executive Office of the President (EOP)—the Council of Economic Advisers (Carter) and the Office of Management and Budget (Reagan)—have spearheaded the effort. As we have already indicated, however, the EOP activities have thus far largely been limited to the lowest level of oversight—namely, the review of individual regulations—and only to those regulations promulgated by regulatory agencies within the executive branch.[11]

The origins of the current executive oversight mechanism can be traced to the Quality of Life Review program instituted in 1971 by the Nixon administration. Directed solely at the regulations issued by the EPA, Quality of Life review subjected draft regulatory proposals by the EPA to interagency comment before they could be published in the *Federal Register*. The process was repeated before the rules were to be promulgated. Disputes were settled at meetings involving the EPA, OMB, and, on some occasions, the White House staff.[12]

The Quality of Life review process was deeply resented by the environmental community, which helped to kill it shortly after the Carter administration assumed office. The major objection to Quality of Life review was that it was fueled primarily by a distaste for environmental regulation. As such, the program hardly fostered a balanced search for more efficient tools or programs. In addition, the actual reviews often did not attract serious attention by the senior-level officials who ran the program.

A less ambitious, but more carefully implemented Execu-

11. The heads of the independent agencies do not report to the President and are therefore not bound by the decisions of the President as implemented through his advisers.

12. For a general description of the Quality of Life Review program, see Harold H. Bruff, "Presidential Power and Administrative Rulemaking," *Yale Law Journal*, January 1979, vol. 88, pp. 464–65.

tive Office program launched by President Ford was the requirement under Executive Order 11821 (November 1974) that executive agencies prepare Inflation Impact Statements.[13] These statements were reviewed by the Council on Wage and Price Stability (CWPS), an office lodged in the Executive Office of the President. Although the reviews helped to stimulate the agencies into taking into account the economic effects of their regulatory actions, and into improving their analytical capabilities to examine those effects, the review process, on balance, does not appear to have significantly affected the substance of the agencies' decisions.[14]

There was deep division in the Carter years over the appropriate degree of regulatory oversight. President Carter's economic advisers strongly advocated the need for involvement by Executive Office officials in important regulatory issues, both to improve analysis and to trim wasteful programs. The agency heads, however, generally objected to the participation by economists in regulatory decision-making, not only to protect their "turf" but, in some cases, because they opposed the use of cost-benefit analysis, or anything remotely similar to it, in reaching regulatory decisions. Moreover, the economic advisers were often clipped by political advisers in the White House, who feared that key constituency groups would be upset if the rules they favored were perceived to be weakened by such review. Ultimately, a strong regulatory oversight program was nullified by President Carter's disinclination to make the reform of social regulations part of his economic program. These impressions, together with those that follow regarding the ineffectiveness of the Carter oversight efforts, are confirmed by President Carter's recent memoirs, which contain no account of

13. The requirements of Executive Order 11821 were updated in December 1976 through Executive Order 11949.

14. See "The Inflation Impact Statement Program: An Assessment of the First Two Years," *American University Law Review,* Summer 1977, pp. 1138–68. The Council found the quality of the statements produced by the agencies to be uneven but also found improvement over time. *Council on Wage and Price Stability Quarterly Report* No. 7 (1976).

his administration's efforts to reform the regulatory process in general and social regulation in particular.[15]

In the end, the administration settled on a compromise procedure that concentrated on improving the inflation impact review process launched under President Ford. One problem perceived with the Ford program was that the inflation analyses performed by the agencies often represented no more than after-the-fact justifications of the rules that were finally issued.[16] Moreover, because few agencies had internal capability to perform the studies, much work was contracted out—and then ignored by agencies poorly equipped to evaluate it.

The Carter administration attempted to reform the process by changing the analysis requirement itself and by widening the participation and heightening the visibility of the review procedure. Through Executive Order 12044, issued in March 1978, executive branch agencies were required to set forth not only the estimates of the economic consequences of each major new regulatory proposal, but the reasons why the proposal was favored over alternatives.[17] To help ensure that the analyses were sufficiently timely and useful to be taken into account by agency decision-makers in deciding upon the final content of their rules, President Carter authorized in late 1977 the creation of the Regulatory Analysis Review Group (RARG), chaired by the Council of Economic Advisers and composed of representatives from the Executive Office and executive departments with major regulatory responsibilities.[18]

15. Jimmy Carter, *Keeping Faith* (New York: Bantam Books, 1982).

16. The environmental impact statement requirement under the National Environmental Policy Act has also been criticized for requiring agencies to prepare little more than after-the-fact justifications of the environmental aspects of their decisions.

17. "Major" regulations were defined as those having an economic impact of over $100 million or a significant qualitative impact on prices and on certain industries and regions of the country. This definition was largely carried over in the Reagan Executive Order (12291), discussed later in this chapter.

18. The total membership included: The Council of Economic Advisers (chair), the Office of Management and Budget, the Office of Science and Technology Policy, the Departments of Agriculture, Commerce, Energy, Health, Education, and Welfare, Housing and Urban Development, Interior,

In contrast to the broad powers held by OMB under the Quality of Life Review program, the authority of RARG was far more limited. First, it was formally chartered to review only the regulatory analyses of agencies and not the substance of the final decisions. Although the line between the content of the analyses and the decisions was blurred, the distinction reinforced the impression among the agencies that RARG's role in regulatory decision-making was to be limited.

Second, RARG was limited by political and staffing constraints to reviewing the regulatory analyses of only ten to twenty major regulatory proposals per year.[19] Bowing to the concerns of particular agencies that they might be over-reviewed, the President also restricted RARG to reviewing no more than four proposals from each agency per year.[20]

Finally, the effectiveness of the RARG process was limited because the agencies were not legally required to adopt its recommendations (although they were required by the Administrative Procedure Act at least to respond to RARG's criticisms). Indeed, the designers and advocates of the process— the President's economic advisers in the EOP—recognized this limitation. Nevertheless, they hoped that key officials in the EOP would urge agency heads and their staffs to examine the suggestions in RARG reports before issuing their final rules. In

---

Justice, Labor, Transportation, Treasury, and the Environmental Protection Agency. A four-member Executive Committee (composed of the CEA, OMB, and two rotating members serving six month terms, one an economic and one a regulatory member) was responsible for choosing the regulatory analyses to be reviewed. Since the regulatory analysis requirement did not extend to the independent agencies, the proposals of such agencies were not subject to RARG review.

19. The reviews were actually written by staff at the CEA and the Council on Wage and Price Stability (CWPS) and were filed in the proposing agency's rulemaking record by the close of the sixty-day public comment period.

20. Although the annual limits, which initially were the center of an interagency tempest before RARG was formally established, were never binding, the fact that they existed in some cases deterred RARG officials from undertaking a review for fear that it would be perceived as an effort to gang up on that agency.

fact, this happened on a regular basis throughout the rest of the Carter administration. On two occasions while we were at CEA, the President himself became involved.

Six RARG reports were completed or were in the process of being prepared through May 1979 (during the period at least one of us was at the CEA). On one other occasion—the "cotton dust" episode—substantial Executive Office involvement in the rulemaking occurred, although no formal RARG report was prepared. Brief summaries of the rules reviewed by RARG, the substance of RARG's comments, and the outcomes of RARG activities are presented in table 4.2.

The RARG reviews of the rules summarized in table 4.2 generally highlighted two questions. First, did the agency adequately balance the incremental costs of its proposals against the incremental benefits? In four of the reviews—those concerning OSHA's acrylonitrile rule, the EPA's ozone and new source performance standards, and Transportation's proposal to provide equal access for the handicapped—RARG suggested that a more reasonable balance between incremental costs and benefits could have been attained through a standard different from the one proposed by the agency. Second, at whatever goal or standard the agency might set, did the agency choose the most cost-effective method of regulation? In all of the cases summarized in the table, RARG concluded that the agency, in fact, had not chosen the least-cost method of attaining its objectives.

As can be seen from table 4.2, RARG had at best modest success in persuading the agencies to modify their proposals to meet these two types of concerns during our tenure at CEA. In only one case—Transportation's equal access for the handicapped rule—did an agency clearly appear to alter its original proposal because of RARG's comments. In three other cases—OSHA's acrylonitrile, the EPA's ozone, Interior's strip mining rules—the proposals were changed in a manner consistent with RARG's recommendations, but the agency denied being influenced by RARG.[21]

21. Agencies, of course, have both political and possibly legal reasons for

Table 4.2. RARG Activities, January 1978 – March 1979

Brief Description of Proposed Rule	Date of RARG Filing	Key Issues Raised by RARG and/or by Executive Office Presidential Advisers	Degree of Post-RARG Executive Office Involvement	Change in Proposal Due to RARG or Post-RARG Activity
1. OSHA's Cotton Dust Rule proposed maximum permissible dust exposure levels to be met primarily through engineering controls in the cotton ginning, milling, and weaving industries	None	Presidential advisers expressed preference for performance standards to be met through any combination of engineering controls, personal protective devices, and work practices	Extentive, including the President	President rejected the views of his advisers, although he lengthened the phase-in period of the standards
2. OSHA's Acrylonitrile Rule proposed three alternative maximum missible acrylonitrile exposure levels	May 1978	Urged that benefits of the various exposure levels be weighed against their cost; recommended different exposure levels for different industries as more cost-effective than uniform standards; suggested that OSHA permit firms flexibility in meeting the standards	Occasional staff-level discussions	Difficult to discern, although the final exposure level chosen was demonstrated by RARG to have been more cost-effective than at least one of the other alternatives; other RARG suggestions were not followed

3. OSHA's Generic Carcinogen Policy proposed a framework for regulating carcinogens in the workplace by establishing a method for categorizing potential carcinogens and fixing a regulatory response applicable to each category	October 1978	Expressed concern that OSHA's proposed scientific principles were not consistent with those of other agencies; also criticized OSHA's proposal to link the classification of potential carcinogens with automatic regulatory responses	Intensive staff-level discussion	Difficult to discern, little apparent change
4. EPA's Revised Ozone Standards proposed revisions in primary ambient air quality standards for photochemical oxidants from 0.08 parts per million (ppm) to 0.10 ppm.	October 1978	Expressed concern about the high annual costs of the 0.10 ppm standard—which could have ranged as high as $18.8 billion—in relation to the benefits; also criticized EPA for not providing an adequate rationale for its choice of the 0.10 ppm standard	Extensive staff- and Cabinet-level discussion and brief discussion with the President.	EPA issued a final primary standard of 0.12 ppm. Appears that RARG influenced outcome.

Table 4.2. RARG Activities, January 1978 – March 1979 (continued)

Brief Description of Proposed Rule	Date of RARG Filing	Key Issues Raised by RARG and/or by Executive Office Presidential Advisers	Degree of Post-RARG Executive Office Involvement	Change in Proposal Due to RARG or Post-RARG Activity
5. Transportation's Equal Access for the Handicapped Rule proposed retrofitting of urban mass transit systems, including both subways and buses	October 1978	Concluded that substitution of an extended bus system for subway retrofit would be substantially more cost-effective	Extensive staff-level discussion	Final rule appeared to pay heed to RARG suggestions by requiring subway retrofits only at "key" stations
6. Interior's Surface Mining Regulations to implement provisions of the Surface Mining and Reclamation Act of 1977	January 1979	Concluded that certain detailed requirements were not cost-effective	Extensive staff- and Cabinet-level discussion	Very minor changes
7. EPA's New Source Performance Standards for Electric Utilities to require a uniform percentage reduction in sulfur emissions from coal burned by electric utilities	March 1979	Criticized uniformity of the percentage reduction requirement applicable to coals of all sulfur content; concluded that alternative emissions requirements would better protect the environment at lower cost	Extensive, up to the President	Adopted a less stringent standard, in part due to RARG

In the most famous case of EOP and presidential oversight, involving OSHA's cotton dust standard, the President's economic advisers were clearly outmaneuvered. As we suggest below, this defeat was particularly important because it came just as the RARG process was getting off the ground. In the cotton dust case, the President himself—after considerable skirmishing between the CEA, the domestic policy staff, and the Department of Labor—rebuffed suggestions by the economists that the stringency of the rule be relaxed. In addition, he rejected the economists' recommendation that the performance-requirements standard be broadened to permit employers to choose their means of compliance between providing their employees with respirators or installing expensive engineering controls. Instead, the President agreed with OSHA that engineering controls were necessary to ensure compliance with the exposure requirements of the rule.[22]

In the period from mid-1979 to January 1981, RARG reviewed proposals in addition to those listed in Table 4.2.[23] While we have no personal knowledge of the outcomes, there is little evidence that the effectiveness of the RARG process in

---

not admitting in public that their decisions were influenced by the advice of White House officials. Nevertheless, even when this tendency is taken into account, the fact that the final rules themselves in each of the above cases did not change materially from the initial proposals indicates that RARG had only limited influence.

22. For another description of the cotton dust case, see Christopher DeMuth, "Constraining Regulatory Costs—Part 1: the White House Programs," *Regulation,* January/February 1980, pp. 13–26.

23. These included the EPA's hazardous waste standards, guidelines for water effluents in the leather tanning industry, and its air carcinogen policy; DOE's building and energy performance standards and its proposed interim and final coal conversion regulations for utilities and industrial boilers; and the HEW's proposal for labeling to accompany prescription drugs. The Council on Wage and Price Stability, by itself, also continued to review the major regulatory proposals of both executive branch and independent agencies. For an official description and assessment of the reviews performed both by RARG and the CWPS, see Thomas D. Hopkins et al., "A Review of the Regulatory Interventions of the Council on Wage and Price Stability" (Washington D.C.: Council on Wage and Price Stability, January 1981).

influencing the direction of regulatory decisions increased during this time. This is hardly surprising, since as the administration's term wore on, the President's attention was increasingly diverted by nonregulatory issues.

In addition, the President's economic advisers, and through them RARG, grew hesitant in the wake of the cotton dust episode about bringing controversial regulatory issues directly to the President's desk. The problem was compounded by the vacillation of the President between encouragement to his economic advisers to "Be Bold" and wariness about the political fallout from boldness—with the latter almost always carrying the day. Since the RARG process contained no incentives for agencies to cooperate or heed RARG's advice, and because RARG could not control any of the levers of power about which agencies really care—appropriations, legislative mandates, appointments or confirmations, fame or enticements beyond the revolving door—it is not surprising that the oversight efforts directed at individual rules during the Carter administration showed only modest success.

The creation of RARG was not the only oversight step taken by the Carter administration. In an effort to provide some oversight at a level higher than that related to reviews of individual rules, President Carter created in 1978 the interagency Regulatory Council.[24] The Council was charged with two major functions: (1) preparation of biannual calendars of major regulatory proposals from agencies throughout the government; and (2) coordination of the development of major regulatory proposals in which more than one agency might have an interest. The second function, in particular, promised to bring for the first time some oversight to the higher level problem of coordinating the regulatory actions of different agencies, if not helping to establish some type of priority-setting mechanism.

The calendar requirement was a useful step. For the first

24. Unlike RARG, the Council included most of the independent regulatory agencies, which participated on a voluntary basis. Agencies and officials within the Executive Office of the President served as advisers to the Council but did not formally belong.

time, the public and all of the various government agencies had a way of knowing in advance what proposals were scheduled. The calendar was also designed to provide projected cost and benefit information for these proposals. In practice, however, little beyond the most rudimentary estimates were generally reported. For example, many cost projections were no more specific than, "The cost of this regulation is expected to exceed $100 million," which was the dollar threshold required for a proposal to be reported in the calendar.[25]

The Regulatory Council also had considerable difficulty performing its second and far more important task: coordinating the development of major regulations. As the staff of the Council soon discovered, heads of regulatory agencies were not accustomed to accounting to their peers for the major policy decisions embodied in their regulatory proposals. Moreover, the titular head of the Council—Douglas Costle, the administrator of the EPA—had enough to handle within his own agency and showed little inclination to impose his own views on the other agencies that belonged to the Council.[26]

25. In addition to its calendar publication efforts, the Council also conducted studies of the impact of regulation on certain industries and sectors of the economy, such as steel and autos.

26. A major early test of the Council's effectiveness came in its attempt to coordinate the development of OSHA's carcinogen policy with the cancer policies of other agencies—primarily the CPSC, EPA, and FDA. OSHA had proposed its policy in an effort to standardize its future regulations of actual or potential carcinogens. Substances were to be classified only on the basis of evidence of their carcinogenicity (potency and exposure were not to be taken into account). The generic proposal then would have required that exposure to those substances classified as potential carcinogens be reduced to the "lowest feasible level" and, if "suitable substitutes" were available, to be banned altogether.

The Council was formed shortly after RARG criticized OSHA's proposal for not including potency and exposure in its classification scheme and for automatically requiring, regardless of the costs and benefits, reductions of exposure to potential carcinogens to the "lowest feasible level." It was understood at the time that OSHA's final cancer policy would not be issued until agreement on a common cancer regulatory policy had been reached among the four relevant agencies.

In the end, however, OSHA issued its final rule in January 1980 substan-

In the end, both RARG and the Regulatory Council were able to achieve only limited success for the same reasons: insufficient authority from the President and a diffusion of responsibility among a large number of agencies. The interagency composition of both groups, while symbolizing some degree of cooperation, in fact represented a formula for ineffectiveness. In the case of RARG, the oversight function could have worked better if the President had given strong and clear support to his economic advisers, but he never did. The problems with the Regulatory Council were more fundamental, since *by design* the President's Executive Office was excluded from membership —providing political distance, to be sure, but also a guarantee that nothing truly important would be entrusted to the Council for resolution.[27]

President Reagan's regulatory advisers clearly recognized the shortcomings of the Carter oversight efforts, for it took the new administration less than one month to abolish both RARG

---

tially unchanged from its original proposal. In particular, the final rule did not permit balancing of costs and benefits, nor did it require a risk assessment, as routinely performed in other agencies, such as the EPA. Since the major purpose of the Regulatory Council's involvement in the development of OSHA's carcinogen policy was to generate a consensus on the use by all agencies of risk assessment techniques, the Council's inability to persuade OSHA to follow a consensus policy was a clear failure. After the Reagan administration assumed office, OSHA Administrator Thorne Auchter announced that the policy adopted in 1980 would be reviewed.

27. Moreover, the circumstances in which the Council was formed help to explain why its role was so limited. The Council was established in the final days before the October 1978 announcement of the President's anti-inflation program. The major part of that program consisted of the wage-price guidelines and the ill-fated real-wage insurance proposal. The idea to form the Council was developed, ironically, not by the regulators, but rather by the President's economic and political advisers, who saw the creation of the Council as a way of broadening the scope of the anti-inflation effort. The regulators revolted, however, at the suggestion made by these advisers that the Council be chaired by the OMB, that the regulatory calendar be prepared by the OMB, and that the President would have veto power over agency proposals. Given this history, it is no surprise that the Council was unable to play a major oversight role. The functions were delegated to the wrong place in a time of hasty decision-making and political compromise.

and the Regulatory Council and to issue a new executive order on federal regulation (12291) to replace the previous Carter order. The Reagan executive order addressed the principal weaknesses of the Carter oversight bodies, their dispersion and lack of authority, by vesting in the OMB unmistakable oversight authority over the regulatory activities of the executive branch agencies.[28] In addition, to give content and direction to this oversight function, the order imposed on the agencies a series of procedural and substantive requirements.[29]

The principal procedural directive of the order requires that executive branch agencies prepare Regulatory Impact Analyses (RIAs) of their major rules.[30] The RIAs must describe the potential benefits and costs of agency proposals and identify those effects that cannot be quantified in monetary terms (section 3(d)). This stops short of requiring the preparation of cost-benefit analyses (in which *all elements* of benefits and costs are expressed in monetary terms) but nevertheless formalizes the previous "regulatory analysis" requirement incorporated in the Carter executive order.[31]

Under the order's substantive requirements, the executive branch agencies are directed, to the extent permitted by law,

28. The order mentions that oversight authority is also vested in a presidential task force on regulatory relief, consisting of the vice president (chair), the director of the OMB, the chairman of the CEA, the President's domestic adviser, and the heads of the Departments of Commerce, Justice, Labor, and Treasury. In practice, however, the OMB runs the daily paper flow and activities of the task force and dominates the decision-making apparatus.

29. The next three pages draw on Michael Sohn and Robert Litan, "The Role of Economic Analysis in the Regulatory Process," *Issues in Bank Regulation,* Winter 1982, pp. 30–36.

30. The definition of "major" rules (at section 1(b)) is substantially the same as under the Carter order. The director of the OMB has the authority to decide whether or not a particular rule is "major" (at section 6(a)(1)).

31. In addition, the order requires the RIAs to contain a description of regulatory alternatives capable of achieving the given regulatory objective at lower cost and an explanation of the *legal reasons* why any such alternative could not be adopted. The first part of this cost-effectiveness requirement is the same as under the Carter order, but the order's requirement that the agency explain the "legal reasons" for not adopting a more cost-effective rule goes beyond the previous requirement.

to issue new regulations only where potential social benefits outweigh potential social costs (section 2(b)). As under the previous Carter order, agencies must choose the regulatory approach that is the most cost-effective of possible alternatives, unless the particular statutory mandate requires otherwise (section 2(d)). The order also requires the agencies to establish regulatory objectives and priorities with the "aim of maximizing the aggregate net benefits to society, taking into account the condition of the particular industries affected . . . the condition of the national economy, and other regulatory actions contemplated for the future" (sections 2(c) and 2(e)).

The OMB now exercises its control over the regulatory process by enforcing these requirements. Specifically, the Reagan order requires the executive branch agencies to submit to the OMB for review new major regulatory proposals together with preliminary RIAs at least sixty days prior to publication of the proposals in the *Federal Register*. If it finds it necessary, the OMB may force a delay in the announcement of a proposal until the issues raised by the review have been resolved. Similarly, the order requires the submission of both the final RIAs and the final rules themselves at least thirty days in advance of the publication of final rules. During this period, the OMB may submit its views to the agencies and prevent the publication of rules until the agencies have incorporated responses to those views in their rulemaking records.

These "pre-clearance" enforcement powers give the Executive Office of the President considerable control over individual rules. Such power extends far beyond the authority of the Carter administration's Regulatory Analysis Review Group. Not only does the order give the Executive Office the authority to oversee individual rules but, at least in theory, it enables the President's advisers to play a major role in the formulation of regulatory priorities through its direction to enforce the requirement that the agencies set their regulatory priorities to, among other things, maximize net social benefits.[32]

32. In addition, section 6(a)(5) grants authority to the OMB and the task force to "identify duplicative, overlapping, and conflicting rules" and to require "appropriate interagency consultation to minimize such duplication, overlap, or conflict."

In practice, however, the order has been aimed primarily at *individual rulemakings,* or the lowest of the three levels of oversight described at the outset of this chapter. Oversight of regulatory priorities, while mentioned in the order, is still largely more a goal than a reality. And no oversight is exercised at the highest level—or the total private-sector impact of regulatory activity. In short, executive oversight of regulation has finally pulled out of the station, but it is a long distance from its final destination.[33]

Inefficiency

The second major defect in today's regulatory process is that it is inefficient. We mean this in the economic sense: that the same quantity of resources presently being devoted to meeting the nation's regulatory objectives could be reallocated to produce a greater level of benefits than the nation is currently receiving. Put another way, the same level of benefits that is now being produced by federal regulatory activities could be achieved through a lower total resource commitment.

It is difficult to compile a large number of examples of inefficiencies resulting from the present system, since the regulatory analysis requirement has been in effect for only a relatively short period, and many of the analyses that have been performed have not contained sufficient information to permit an informed comparison of the cost-effectiveness of the rules that have been promulgated. Nevertheless, some striking evidence of the inefficiency both across and within regulatory programs and agencies is illustrated by the cost estimates of saving lives through different federal programs presented in table 2.1 (chapter 2). The differences in the table are striking, ranging from $166,000 to save a life through kidney dialysis to

33. For recent reviews of the Reagan executive oversight efforts, see George Eads, "Harnessing Regulation: the Evolving Role of White House Oversight," *Regulation,* May/June 1981, pp. 19–26; Christopher C. DeMuth, "A Strong Beginning," *Regulation,* January/February 1982, pp. 15–18; and Marvin Kosters and Jeffrey Eisenach, "Is Regulatory Relief Enough?" *Regulation,* March/April 1982, pp. 20–27.

tens of millions of dollars to save a life by regulating worker exposure to coke oven emissions or acrylonitrile. Within the narrower class of activity represented by federal regulation, there are also wide variations in costs per life saved, from millions to save a life in the workplace to $180,000 to save a life by requiring automobile manufacturers to install air bags or automatic seat belts. Clearly, the life-saving objectives of these programs and regulations could be advanced in a far more efficient manner by shifting resources away from the high-cost-per-life programs and rules to those where lives can be saved on the margin with fewer resources.

The inefficiencies are also present *within* regulatory programs and agencies. We saw this time and again during the course of our regulatory oversight duties at CEA. For example, within the EPA's air quality program, the ambient air quality standard for ozone was several times less cost-beneficial on the margin than the similar standard set for lead, which in turn was an order of magnitude less effective than OSHA's workplace lead standard. Even more striking are disparities within the same regulatory program, such as the set of the EPA's new source performance standards for particulates, which impose marginal costs per metric ton ranging from (in 1978 dollars) $259 for some types of pulp mills to $5,500 for light-duty diesel vehicles, the CWPS estimate for the cost of compliance with 1983 diesel standards.[34] Similar disparities between the motor vehicle and stationary source emission programs can be found in the incremental costs of controlling other pollutants.[35] Finally, as clearly indicated in table 2.1, the stringency of various OSHA standards could be readjusted, if the law permitted, to produce a more efficient result.

There may be good reasons for such differences in incremental costs both within and between regulatory programs and

34. Lawrence J. White, *The Regulation of Air Pollutant Emissions from Motor Vehicles* (Washington, D.C.: American Enterprise Institute, 1982).

35. See Lawrence J. White, *Reforming Regulations: Processes and Problems* (Englewood Cliffs, N.J.: Prentice-Hall, 1981), p. 109. In the course of our participation in the EPA's "sulfur scrubbing" rule, we observed similar variations in the marginal costs of controlling sulfur dioxide (through new source performance standards) across industries.

in relation to other governmental and private activities. Some of the differences in the costs per life saved across different programs, for example, can be attributed to differences in attributes of the populations (e.g., age, sex, attitudes toward risk, etc.) protected by the various regulatory programs. Similarly, society can justifiably spend more in reducing risks to which people are involuntarily exposed, such as air pollution from industry smokestacks, than in reducing risks people voluntarily and willingly accept, such as those posed by cigarette smoking.[36] Yet while such reasons may help to explain some of the variation in incremental costs across different programs, we do not believe they can explain all of it given that, as indicated in table 2.1, the costs per life of different regulatory programs vary by factors of 10 to 100.

As we discuss in greater detail below, we believe there are two basic reasons why the nation's current regulatory effort is not more efficient. The first, which is related to the inadequacy of the higher levels of oversight already examined, is the absence of an overall budget constraint on total private sector expenditures mandated by federal regulations. More precisely, the regulatory process is economically wasteful primarily because decision-makers are not forced to choose among competing programs within a limited budget. Although they must work within the constraints of their statutory powers and broad social consensus, regulators are typically given blank checks to choose whatever expenditure of private costs of compliance they see fit. This unlimited line of credit on the private purse makes regulators unique in our mixed economy. One of the keys to regulatory reform is the tightening of the constraints on regulators so that they respond better and more efficiently to national priorities.

36. See Richard Wilson and Edmund Crouch, *Risk/Benefit Analysis* (Cambridge, Mass.: Ballinger, 1982). Wilson and Crouch devote considerable attention to quantifying and comparing the risks of different activities and assessing the differences in resources devoted to reducing those various risks. They, too, find wide disparities among different programs in incremental resources devoted to saving a life—ranging from as little as $34,000, required by traffic safety improvements, to $22 million by coal mine safety standards, and as high as $1 billion through nuclear waste requirements.

A second source of inefficiency, paradoxically in contrast to the lack of an overall budget constraint on regulatory decision-making, arises from *too much* restriction on the freedom of agencies to balance costs against benefits and to choose from among a variety of regulatory and nonregulatory techniques. Such restrictions not only inhibit agencies from reaching cost-effective solutions to individual regulatory problems, but frustrate any attempts to rationalize the allocation of resources across regulatory programs and agencies. These "micro" sources of inefficiency are examined below following our discussion of the "macro" problems arising from the lack of overall budgetary discipline.

1. The Absence of a Budget Process for Regulation

Budgets or budgetlike constraints are pervasive throughout the American economy. Consumers face budget constraints in allocating their incomes; businesses face financial and cash flow constraints in their investment and production decisions; the federal government contends with the macroeconomic constraints of unemployment and inflation in setting overall levels of taxes and expenditures; many states and localities are constrained by constitutional limits on deficits; and the nation as a whole contends with the harsh judgment of foreign exchange markets when imports exceed exports.

Budgets are necessary because resources are limited. This is most evident to individuals and firms in a market economy. Thus, the classical economic view of consumers is that they choose how to allocate a limited income and stock of assets between alternative goods and savings in order to achieve maximum satisfaction. In the process, consumers perform two critical functions, deciding first *how much* to spend during a given period and then how to *allocate* this total among alternative uses. A similar two-level budget problem must constantly be solved by profit-maximizing firms.

The constraints imposed by the market are less evident to governments, which can use coercion to collect taxes and can simply borrow money to finance expenditures. True, macroeconomic and political forces place some upper limit on government spending, but these constraints are inherently much looser than the income and asset constraints facing private individuals and firms.

The federal government had no tighter constraints during the first 145 years of the republic, since no overall federal budget process existed. Instead, Congress primarily concerned itself with the legality of expenditures, and not with developing a budget. Arthur Smithies described the system this way:

> It is a striking fact that, despite occasional lip service to the idea in public speeches and Congressional resolutions, nineteenth-century budgetary arrangements did practically nothing that was effective to promote economy and efficiency in government. The detailed appropriation system obstructed economizing rather than promoted it; the revenue sanction on extravagance was extraordinarily weak and the accounting system was designed to achieve other objectives. Furthermore, the Executive was so weakened by the Congress' assumption of exclusive power that there were few opportunities for the President to take the initiative with economizing measures.[37]

It took over sixty years to develop a federal budget process, beginning in 1911 with a study of an executive budget that led to the passage of the Budget Act of 1921.

The 1921 act contained three pathbreaking features. First, it required the President to submit a comprehensive expenditure and revenue budget to Congress. This quickly assured, for the first time, that the Executive would be forced not only to weigh competing alternatives, but also to determine the new taxes, loans, or other appropriate actions needed to meet the estimated budget deficit. Second, the act provided the President an institutional framework for setting budget priorities by establishing a "Bureau of the Budget" (now the OMB) directly responsible to the President. A sizable and talented staff loyal to

---

37. Arthur Smithies, *The Budgetary Process in the United States* (New York: McGraw-Hill, 1955), pp. 65ff. See also Louis Fisher, "The Authorization-Appropriation Process in Congress: Formal Rules and Informal Practices," *Catholic University Law Review* 29:51–105.

the President was integral to providing hope for an effective budget process. The final major feature of the 1921 act was the creation of a General Accounting Office (GAO). This office was made responsible for reviewing and auditing the budget accounts, but (contrary to the recommendations of the Taft Commission and other experts) was placed outside the executive branch.

The 1921 act fundamentally transformed the operation of the federal government. Yet it left one gaping hole by excluding Congress from the requirement to set overall revenue and expenditure targets. Not surprisingly, despite the discipline the act imposed on the President, Congress subsequently and frequently frustrated the effort by adding expenditures to the budget.

Congress finally took action to remedy this defect by passing the Budget Act of 1974. Under this act, Congress now receives the President's recommendations and sets expenditure ceilings, both overall and as to major items, for each fiscal year. Of particular importance is that Congress created centralized budget committees in the Senate and House to implement the budget requirements as well as a new Congressional Budget Office to provide analytical support.

In short, the nation has had some type of budget process for controlling and allocating its direct government expenditures for over sixty years. By contrast, *no steps have yet been taken to establish a corresponding budget process for federal regulation.* Compared to the institutionalized control of the federal expenditure process, therefore, the regulatory process is "immature" and at least six decades behind.

Specifically, four steps central to bringing the expenditure process under control are missing from the current regulatory process. First, neither the Executive nor the Congress systematically determines the overall level of regulatory activity in a given period. Second, no office in the executive branch or committee in Congress is responsible for systematically establishing regulatory priorities across the government. Third, the Executive has not instituted any systematic process of submitting regulatory proposals or efforts to the Congress. Finally, there is no office to audit regulatory programs. In sum, no control mechanism exists for regulation that requires decision-makers throughout the government to confront explicitly and to solve the two-level budget problem, which is routinely addressed by private actors and by the federal government itself in its direct expenditure activities.

We are under no illusion in making the comparison between the current regulatory and federal expenditure processes that the existing expenditure budget procedure is flawless and must serve therefore as an ideal model for creating a parallel regulatory budget process. There are recognized and important differences between public and private budgets that impede the effectiveness of *any* public budget procedure. As indicated above, for example, governments are subject to less severe overall spending constraints than private individuals and firms. Perhaps even more important, the two-level budget problem confronting the government is decided not by the consumers of public services, but rather by their elected representatives in the executive and legislative branches. As is well-documented in the political theory literature,[38] this reduces the quality of information available to decision-makers and permits, and perhaps encourages, the formation of coalitions that may operate to prevent the resulting budget allocations from being efficient in the classical economic sense. More recently, concerns have been raised about whether the current expenditure budget process can survive the political tensions created in the wake of the Reagan administration's supply-side gamble to force large expenditure reductions through prior cuts in tax rates.

That the existing budget process is not ideal does not mean that it is without economic value. Budgeting is a process that has important substantive effects. By forcing decision-makers to debate and decide which programs contribute most to the

38. See Anthony Downs, *An Economic Theory of Democracy* (New York: Harper and Row, 1957); Aaron Wildavsky, *The Politics of the Budgetary Process* (Boston: Little Brown, 1964); David Mayhew, *Congress: The Electoral Connection* (New Haven: Yale University Press, 1974); Thomas Mann, *Unsafe at Any Margin* (Washington, D.C.: American Enterprise Institute, 1980).

public welfare, the budget process raises the fundamental questions of resource allocation that would otherwise not have to be addressed, let alone decided. If the resulting decisions are not as efficient as publicly desired, the solution is to strengthen the mechanism of control, not to abandon the process altogether.[39]

The current budget process also serves an important political function, especially now that Congress has made itself an equal participant with the Executive in the process. From the time of James Madison through the present, a principal function of the government has been to respond to the demands of a wide variety of factions, or interest groups. Without a budget process, the Executive and legislature would find it easier to cater to the expenditure demands of the multitude of interest groups that constantly seek government assistance. The expenditure budget imposes a discipline that forces the President and the Congress to weigh the relative merits of the competing claims. This is particularly true now that so much authority has been transferred away from the many congressional committees —each with its own special interests and projects—and vested in the powerful budget committees charged with broader government-wide responsibilities.

As a result, the federal expenditure budget process has created vital institutional incentives for the individual members of the budget committees and for the Congress as a whole to understand, care about, and *vote on* the macroscopic budget issues of central importance to the voting public. These educational and decision-making functions are vital in a democ-

39. *See, e.g.,* the debate between Louis Fisher, Robert N. Giaimo, Phillip S. Hughes, and Alice M. Rivlin in *The Brookings Bulletin,* Spring 1981, pp. 6–13. *See also* Allen Schick, *Congress and Money* (Washington, D.C.: The Urban Institute, 1980); Alice M. Rivlin, ''Congress and the Budget Process,'' *Challenge,* March/April 1981, pp. 31–37. It bears emphasis that apart from the few legislators who favor scrapping entirely the heart of the current budget process (the reconciliation procedure), the other suggestions for reform would essentially leave the existing process intact, if not make it stronger. Suggestions in the latter category include proposals to eliminate the first budget resolution (which now only sets budget goals), to stretch the entire process out over two years instead of one, and to require a three-fifths vote for approval of higher expenditure ceilings than those recommended by the budget committees.

racy—whether or not they always lead to an "efficient" result—for they require elected representatives and ultimately the voting public to consider fundamental political issues in the proper framework of what can be afforded, given limited resources and the commitments made to the pursuit of other programs.

Because these incentives are absent in the regulatory sphere, there is no such political debate about the regulatory activities of the federal government. No one addresses the question of how much, in the aggregate, the nation can afford—or should spend—to meet regulatory objectives. Similarly, virtually no debate occurs on which regulatory programs deserve highest priority. Instead, regulatory issues are addressed piecemeal, outside of any larger, macroscopic context.

The problems with the current regulatory effort can be usefully compared to those of the market in the face of undesirable externalities. As we discussed in the last chapter, an externality arises when the social cost or benefit of an activity does not accrue to the decision-maker. The classic example is where a steel firm spews out soot and does not pay for the resulting health and property damages. Under these circumstances, a profit-conscious firm will use too little capital and labor and too much clean air in its productive process.

Enter the environmental regulator charged with "cleaning up the mess." The problem is that the regulator has exactly the opposite incentive from that of the firm: the regulator is accountable for the dirty air but not for the capital and labor that the steel firm must spend to clean the air. *Thus, regulators generate their own externalities: they impose costs on other entities, firms and consumers, and do not need to spend their own resources in meeting the regulation.* In the absence of a mechanism that forces regulators to "internalize" these costs, they will engage in regulatory activities that require too much private expenditure for the results achieved.

2. Poor Management: Unrealistic Goals and Constraints on Balancing
Even if all federal regulatory activity were subject to an effec-

tive overall resource constraint, the efficiency of the regulatory effort would continue to be impeded by various statutes which, to varying degrees, commit regulators to unrealistic objectives by constraining their abilities to balance costs against benefits in making regulatory decisions.

Each regulatory action requires a decision whether to regulate, how to regulate, and the appropriate level of regulatory stringency. Efficiency requires at each point that the overall benefits from the effort be compared with the costs. Regulation should occur, therefore, only when the total benefits outweigh the total costs. The type of regulation should be chosen that attains the highest net benefit. And the stringency of the regulation should be increased only as long as the incremental benefits are greater than the incremental costs.

There are certain well-known statutory impediments to such balancing of costs against benefits, however, that inhibit the efficient allocation of resources toward meeting regulatory objectives. In analyzing these statutory constraints, it is useful to distinguish between two types of balancing requirements: (1) *process* laws or directives requiring administrative agencies to prepare formal *analyses* of the costs and benefits involved (in order to inform the decision-maker); and (2) *substantive* laws permitting or requiring agencies to balance costs and benefits in making their regulatory *decisions.*

The matrix in table 4.3 illustrates that balancing may either be required, permitted, or prohibited in analyzing and then deciding upon regulatory alternatives. Conceptually, the approaches to balancing at the analysis and decision-making stages are distinct; in some cases, however, they may turn out to be identical in practice. For example, if a regulatory agency is required by its organic statute to balance costs against benefits in rendering its final regulatory decisions, the agency clearly must also prepare analyses of costs and benefits to support those decisions. The corollary does not hold, however; requiring the agencies to prepare analyses of costs and benefits—in the mold of the recent Carter and Reagan executive orders—does not translate into a requirement that the agencies take such analyses into account in making their regulatory decisions.

Table 4.3. Balancing Used in Regulatory Decision-Making

		Is There a Substantive Requirement That Costs and Benefits Be Balanced in Setting a Regulation?		
		1 Balancing Prohibited	2 Balancing Permitted	3 Balancing Mandatory
Is There a Procedural Requirement That Analysis Is to Be Performed?	A. Analysis Prohibited			
	B. Analysis Permitted			
	C. Analysis Mandatory			

In fact, federal legislation now restricts or impedes several administrative agencies from taking proper account of costs and benefits in their regulatory decisions. A few statutes totally deny agency officials the discretion to weigh costs and benefits. In addition, in many areas there is substantial confusion about the extent to which agencies should weigh the costs and benefits involved in the exercise of their power.

We have not made an exhaustive search of statutes, but we have identified in table 4.4 important statutes where balancing is either prohibited or ambiguous. A more complete list of the balancing requirements in various regulatory statutes is provided in Appendix C. Two significant statutes that totally prohibit balancing are: (1) the provisions in the Clean Air Act that require the EPA to set its ambient air quality standards without regard to costs; and (2) the Delaney clause (of the food and drug laws), which absolutely prohibits the use of food additives that are determined to be carcinogenic in animals. As indicated in table 4.4, the balancing requirements in a host of other statutes are vague and, in practice, have frequently inhibited the rele-

Table 4.4. Important Regulatory Statutes Where Balancing of
Costs and Benefits Is Prohibited or Questionable

Generally held to prohibit balancing

The Delaney clause of the Food, Drug, and Cosmetic Act (a source of
concern with respect to saccharine and nitrites).

National Ambient Air Quality Standards of the Clean Air Act (sources
of concern are ozone, particulates, sulfur oxides, etc.).

Ambiguity on balancing

OSHA's toxic substances regulation (subject of concern for coke
ovens, carcinogens).

Mine Safety Toxic Materials (subject of concern in regulating coal
mines).

Atomic Energy Act (regulation of nuclear power).

Clean Water Standards (estimated to have required up to $60 billion in
capital costs over 1972–83 period).

Noise Emission Standards (may require stringent noise controls in
transportation).

Several energy and transportation safety acts have unclear
provisions.

---

vant agencies from engaging in a serious comparison of costs
and benefits before taking regulatory action.

The restrictions and ambiguities with respect to balancing
are generally reflected in the broad statements of policy that the
agencies are charged to pursue. Consider, for example, the
extremely broad policy direction provided by three recent regulatory statutes:

> The purposes of this title [the Clean Air Act] are (1) to protect and
> enhance the quality of the nation's air resources so as to promote
> the public health and welfare and the productive capacity of its
> population. . . .

> The objective of this act [the Federal Water Pollution Control Act]
> is to restore and maintain the chemical, physical, and biological
> integrity of the nation's waters. . . .

> The Congress declares it to be its purpose and policy . . . to assure
> so far as possible every working man and woman in the nation safe
> and healthful working conditions and to preserve our human
> resources. . . . [Occupational Safety and Health Act].

Such language elevates the chosen regulatory objective to an absolute—a goal to be attained regardless of the costs imposed or of the effects that may be imparted to other objectives. In some cases, of course, society has decided to do precisely that or, in Arthur Okun's words, to put certain institutions outside the "domain of dollars."[40] There are sound reasons, for example, not to allow economic costs to compromise our abhorrence of slavery, our commitment to freedom of speech, or the prohibition of a market in votes. But to impose an absolute imperative against carcinogenic food additives, health risks to workers, or unhealthful environmental exposure to ozone? Such an idea mocks serious political discourse. If we will not allow *any* risks on ozone, how can we allow smoking in public? Why is our health budget limited but our regulatory budget limitless? How can we reconcile a zero-risk philosophy when there are no safe levels of exposure? And, to be realistic, how can we hold such a position when the implication may be that *our entire national income* should be spent on pursuing absolute safety?

There are no satisfactory answers to these questions. A zero-risk philosophy is in fact an anachronism dating from a time when regulatory costs were modest and the wastes in a high-spending philosophy were tolerable. Neither of these holds true today.

The decision to balance rejects zero-risk decision-making. It does not mean, however, that decision-makers must rely mechanically on cost-benefit analysis, as some critics have suggested.[41] Such a prospect—the specter of Corps of Engineers-style hanky panky run wild—must send a chill down the spine of any sensible person. Cost-benefit analysis is a tool to help decision-makers sort out the consequences of a given set of actions. The results of that analysis then form part of the overall package of information from which decision-makers can

40. Arthur Okun, *Equality vs. Efficiency: The Big Tradeoff* (Washington, D.C.: The Brookings Institution, 1976).

41. See, e.g., *Cost-Benefit Analysis: Wonder Tool or Mirage,* Report by the Subcommittee on Interstate and Foreign Commerce. 96th Congress (December 1980). For a recent discussion of this subject, see Marguerite Connerton and Mark McCarthy, *National Policy Papers,* No. 4 (Washington, D.C.: National Policy Exchange, October 1982).

make intelligent choices. The fear that the quantifiable information will always predominate in the decision-making—a Gresham's law of regulation that bad numbers will drive out good sense—is not an argument against sound balancing but against poor decision-making.

In sum, sensible regulation, and indeed reasoned decision-making of any type, requires choice among alternatives. Those statutes that inhibit such choices should be modified to permit the Congress, the Executive, and the agencies to pursue all of the nation's regulatory objectives in a rational and cost-effective manner.

3. Inefficient Regulatory Techniques

The third source of inefficiency arises from the manner in which individual regulations are designed, and particularly from the lack of incentives those regulations give to private firms and individuals to comply through the most cost-effective means available. Because this subject has been studied extensively by other researchers,[42] we confine our discussion here to a brief analysis of how the incentive structure of several recent regulatory decisions could be improved.

In order to make our central point, it is useful to track back over earlier ground. In chapter 3, we noted that the government can accomplish its goals through a wide variety of techniques (see table 3.1). But why, in any particular case, is a regulatory response chosen as a way of attaining a given objective? As we suggested in chapter 3, regulatory responses in a large number of cases arise because political actors find it necessary in the face of a perceived problem simply "to do something." Consider the following examples:

1. When OPEC raised world oil prices in 1973–74, price controls were imposed on domestic oil prices to prevent oil companies from receiving windfall profits.

42. See e.g., Alan V. Kneese and Charles L. Schultze, *Pollution, Prices, and Public Policy* (Washington, D.C.: The Brookings Institution, 1975); Charles L. Schultze, *The Public Use of the Private Interest* (Washington, D.C.: The Brookings Institution, 1977); Eugene Bardach and Robert Kagan, *Social Regulation: Strategies For Reform* (Berkeley, California: Institute for Contemporary Studies, 1982).

2. Because of the energy crisis, and in order to improve fuel efficiency of automobiles, automobile companies were required to attain certain numerical fuel efficiency standards.

3. In order to provide room for economic growth in areas where air quality was cleaner than required, certain permissible increments to pollution were offered to firms on a "first come, first served" basis.

4. When sulfur was found to be dangerous to human health, strict quantitative limits on emissions were imposed, and in some cases particular technologies were mandated.

5. Because of perceived dangers to coal miners' safety, a large number of specific work and design practices were imposed on the underground coal industry.

6. When saccharine was found to induce cancer in animals, it was temporarily banned as a food additive.

Two themes run through this diverse set of regulatory actions. First, the political or regulatory decision-makers determined that there were defects in the private market and/or distributional implications that were sufficiently grave to be remedied through government intervention. In some cases, such as air pollution control, the necessity of government involvement was not controversial. In others, such as the saccharine case or oil price controls, the opposition to government action was widespread.

Second, in each of the examples, the regulatory decisions consisted of specific directives to take actions or desist from particular activities, rather than encouraging the attainment of the goals through the use of generalized incentives permitting firms and individuals to comply in any way they saw fit. The decisions in every case displayed a profound distrust of market mechanisms and a belief that central decision-makers could make better allocation or pricing decisions than could markets. We characterize such a regulatory philosophy, which simply orders that which is broken to be fixed, as the "lawyer-regulator's approach" to regulation.

Economists have long criticized the lawyer's approach. In the early 1900s, the British economist A. C. Pigou suggested that taxes, and not specific government commands, be used to discourage harmful activities. More thoughtful suggestions have emerged since with the growth of the regulatory industry, both inside and outside of government. For example, former CEA Chairman Charles Schultze has led a well-known attack upon command-and-control regulation, favoring instead the use of market-type incentives to induce private agents to produce socially desirable results. In addition, numerous studies have examined the relative efficiency of price-type and command-and-control-type regulations; these tend to confirm that there are significant inefficiencies in the latter, for reasons discussed shortly.[43] We label this use of pricelike devices, rather than legal commands, the "economist-regulator's approach" to regulation.

The economist-regulator would design very different regulatory solutions to the six problems listed above:

1. In order to prevent oil producers from reaping windfall profits through deregulation, a "wellhead" or "windfall profits" tax could be levied on oil producers.

2. To improve fuel efficiency, gasoline itself could be heavily taxed.

3. Rather than being given away to those standing first in line, pollution increments could be auctioned to the highest bidder.

4. Instead of mandated emission limits or technologies, fees (or taxes) could be placed on sulfur emissions.

5. Coal mining companies could be required to purchase large amounts of life and accident insurance for their employees, inducing safe work practices. This need not duplicate workmen's compensation, which provides very limited coverage and, in any case, is not based on the safety experiences of particular firms. Alternatively, stiff fines could be imposed on companies having poor safety records.

6. The appropriate market correction for possible carcinogenic food additives would first be to assure appropriate information and labeling. If such actions were deemed insufficient to protect people from the possible carcinogenic properties of saccharine, artificial and natural sweeteners could be subject to taxation proportional to estimated toxicity. Such taxes would induce lower consumption of the riskier substances and reward companies that found safer substitutes.

43. See Schultze, *op. cit.*

The first suggestion was actually implemented during the Carter administration. The second and third suggestions have been adopted in a limited form. The fourth approach has been actively considered, while the last two strategies are more speculative, but probably feasible.

Economists typically favor the use of pricelike incentive systems, such as those just listed, over direct commands or controls for four reasons.

First, properly functioning markets have remarkable efficiency properties. This can be illustrated by a simplified example involving pollution abatement. Putting aside locational differences, efficient reductions of pollution requires that sources reduce their emissions until the incremental costs of further reduction are equal across all polluters. Under a command-and-control type of regulatory approach, such a rule is virtually impossible to enforce with more than a handful of sources, so the lawyer-regulators typically turn to emissions limitations on major classes of sources. A price system, however, can lead to the efficient rule by increasing the costs of pollution to producers, thereby providing incentives to reduce emissions to the point where the incremental cost of emissions control equals any fee.

Second, market-based systems are much more likely to encourage innovation than direct regulation. Private research and development are generally directed toward those areas where money can be made or saved. If pollution charges became expensive, as they would in price-type systems, then firms could be expected to devote resources to reducing emissions or to designing equipment or techniques that were less polluting. The lawyer's approach, by contrast, could actually be perverse. Since firms are often required to install "best available control technology," they have strong incentives to avoid producing a more effective and expensive control device for fear it will be required.

A third desirable feature of the market approach is that it provides a way to decentralize decisions about how much regulation to impose. The lawyer-regulator substitutes centralized decisions on technology for decentralized choices. Because there is simply no other way to assure compliance, uniform national standards almost always emerge. Under market-type regulation, individual firms would be free to choose their control level (subject only to verification and audit), taking into account differences in firms' technologies, knowledge, costs, and objectives.

Finally, markets allow very difficult distributional decisions to be made in an impersonal but orderly way. In any dynamic economy, there is a continuous reshuffling of fortunes among firms and workers, regions and industries. Every day, tens of thousands of workers lose their jobs or are rehired; some are impoverished while others become rich. The governmental process, however, has enormous difficulty accepting such turmoil as a result of positive legislative action. As a result, regulation is often accompanied by poorly designed egalitarian baggage that frustrates the regulation's purpose or introduces yet new complications. That markets are heartless is actually a plus, for they can accomplish major structural change when it is necessary.

The four features of markets discussed above, which are put in stark and oversimplified terms, are generally qualified in the professional literature. Yet taken as a whole, and given the dismal economic performance over the last ten years, a dispassionate observer may fairly conclude that the rise of increasingly stringent command-and-control techniques as a method of regulation has poorly served the American economy.

As we indicated in chapter 3, the commands and controls are gradually being removed from economic regulation. Over the last five years, regulation has been eliminated or is currently being phased out for oil, natural gas, brokerage fees, airlines, cable TV, and most financial institutions. Judging by the costs of economic regulations reviewed in that chapter, this should lead to a significant reduction in the regulatory burden.

In the area of social regulation, on the other hand, the lawyer-regulator's approach continues to have the upper hand. During the four years of the Carter administration, there were few attempts to introduce pricelike incentives into social regulation, and several command-and-control-type regulations were either strengthened or introduced for the first time. Further, as we document in the next chapter, the antiregulatory zeal of the Reagan administration has thus far proved to be "Ralph Nader run in reverse," producing an arbitrary rollback of rules rather than instituting significant process reforms.

In sum, there are inefficiencies plaguing the current regulatory effort at each stage at which oversight could be exercised. Because there is no constraint mechanism applicable to the total level of private expenditures mandated by regulation, neither elected officials nor regulators have incentives to accomplish their overall regulatory missions in a cost-effective manner. The lack of an overall budget constraint, coupled with statutory constraints on balancing, provides no incentives to decision-makers at the appropriate levels to debate and establish regulatory priorities. And the choice of inefficient responses and regulatory techniques impedes the cost-effectiveness of individual rules. It is unfortunate, as we suggest in the next chapter, that the regulatory reform proposals that have thus far received the most public attention would generally do little to correct any of these problems.

5

Recent Regulatory Reform Proposals

The recent growth in regulatory activity has spawned interest from all political quarters in streamlining the regulatory process and in improving the public accountability of the regulatory agencies. There is no shortage of suggestions. A number of reform initiatives are now being considered by the Congress or have received a significant degree of public attention. In this chapter, we examine the major proposals against the background of the problems identified in the previous chapter. The proposals fall into three categories: (1) those that would reverse the overdelegation of authority to the regulatory agencies, (2) those addressing inefficiencies in particular regulations, and (3) the Reagan administration's strategy of providing "regulatory relief" or simply rolling back the scale of the entire regulatory effort.

Reversing the Delegation of Authority to the Regulatory Agencies

We, of course, are not the first to suggest a need to redress the overdelegation of regulatory authority to the administrative agencies. A variety of elected officials, judges, and analysts have voiced the same concern. There is much less agreement, however, as to who should take on a greater share of regulatory responsibilities. Some have suggested that if the source of the problem is too much delegation by Congress, then Congress itself should reassert authority in the area. The American Bar Association has recommended that the appropriate remedy lies in enhanced presidential control over the regulatory process. Many in the Senate, led by Senator Bumpers of Arkansas, have suggested that the difficulties arising from overdelegation could be cured by tighter judicial scrutiny of administrative decisions. Finally, others argue that there should simply be less regulatory activity.

Despite the wide differences among these proposals, all share the objective of reducing the power of the regulatory agencies. The difficulty, we shall argue, arises because none would do so by establishing a systematic process of review that would require decision-makers in *both* political branches of government to compare the costs and benefits of different regulatory programs and to make tradeoffs among those programs within and across agencies.

1. Reasserting Congressional Authority

In many ways, the most obvious remedies are those that call for an enhanced congressional role in the regulatory process. If regulators are deemed to have too much discretion, it is only because Congress has permitted it. Moreover, to the extent that regulatory decisions require the resolution of fundamental political issues, what better branch of government to resolve those issues than the Congress?

There is a difference of opinion, however, as to the point in the regulatory process where it would be most appropriate for Congress to attempt to reassert its delegated authority. At one extreme are suggestions that Congress start at the beginning of the process by filling in the blank checks in any statutory authorizations that are excessively vague. At the other are proposals to have Congress play a greater role at the end of the process, by empowering itself to veto final agency decisions before they take effect.

Tightening up the vague and often loosely worded statutory delegations of regulatory authority has been favored in some legal circles as the appropriate means by which Congress can correct the current imbalance. As the Court of Appeals for the

District of Columbia recently held in striking down the constitutionality of the legislative veto: "If Congress has given away too much power, *it may by statute take it back or may in the future enact more specific delegations"* (emphasis added).[1] A similar theme was struck in Justice Rehnquist's dissenting opinion in the Benzene case, which argued that the "feasibility" requirement applicable to OSHA's toxic exposure standards was too incomprehensible to be a constitutionally valid delegation.[2]

Although correcting specific regulatory charters has a strong surface appeal, it does not resolve the overdelegation problem. After such modifications are made, it is unlikely that legislators would become involved in regulatory decisions on a more regular basis. This is likely to be particularly true where Congress has deliberately restricted the agencies in some manner from balancing costs against benefits, posing a difficulty not of too *much* agency discretion, but too *little*. To correct this problem solely by expanding the agencies' ability to balance would thus aggravate the real concern raised by delegation in the first instance—the transfer of decision-making responsibility for fundamental political issues from the political to the bureaucratic arena.[3] Put another way, if the necessary amendments to statutes that now inhibit balancing were, in fact,

---

1. Consumer Energy Council of America v. FERC, 673 F.2d 425 (D.C. Cir. 1982).

2. Industrial Union Department, AFL-CIO v. American Petroleum Institute, 448 U.S. 607 (1980) (J. Rehnquist, Dissenting Op.). For a criticism of Rehnquist's opinion, see Antonin Scalia, "A Note on the Benzene Case," *Regulation,* July/August 1980, pp. 25–28. In particular, Scalia (who recently was appointed to the U.S. Court of Appeals for the District of Columbia Circuit) argues that the revival of the "delegation" doctrine by the courts would lead to further judicial activism, given the inherent vagueness of the doctrine. Indeed, it was precisely for this reason—that the boundaries of the doctrine are impossible to define—that the Supreme Court abandoned it in the mid-1930s.

3. A possible exception is the suggestion that the FTC's sweeping authority to promulgate rules defining "unfair and deceptive" trade practices be circumscribed by a cost-benefit test. The present authority of the Commission to set such rules under Section 5 of the FTC Act is so broad that the addition of virtually any type of provision would narrow the agency's discretion.

implemented, there would be an even greater need for an institutional mechanism that would increase the political accountability of the regulatory agencies.

Indeed, there is strong reason for believing that without the systematic involvement of elected officials in making regulatory decisions, the political constituencies supporting the necessary statutory changes simply will not be formed. The recent reluctance of the Reagan administration to amend the Clean Air Act to permit balancing illustrates the difficulties that such amendments have in drawing political support.[4] The reasons are not hard to understand. Since no mechanism now exists to force elected decision-makers to make tradeoffs between regulatory objectives, support for reopening a particular statute can easily be characterized as an attempt to weaken that statute. Even a modest proposal to permit agencies greater freedom to make tradeoffs in reaching regulatory decisions, therefore, can be made to appear as promoting dirty air or unsafe workplaces. If, instead, congressmen were able to tell their constituents that the pursuit of cleaner air must be balanced against safer disposal of toxic wastes—just as Congress must now choose between defense and social programs in authorizing federal expenditures—the difficult political issues involved in amending restrictive statutes would be easier to face.

The political problems of introducing greater flexibility in regulatory charters could be circumvented, of course, through amendments that would clearly *narrow* agency discretion. This would respond directly to the concerns of those who believe that Congress has delegated too much authority to the agencies. For example, Congress itself has set fuel economy and emissions standards for automobiles. Alternatively, it can withdraw agency jurisdiction altogether, as the Congress did with the FTC in revising the FTC's authority to investigate the insurance

---

4. *1982 Economic Report of the President,* pp. 143–46. Similarly, the administration's proposed amendment to the Clean Water Act did not include revisions of the strict best available technology (BAT) emissions requirements to permit some degree of balancing of costs and benefits.

industry and children's advertising and prohibiting the agency from issuing rules in the area of unfair advertising.[5]

The major defect in proposals to substitute congressional for agency decision-making, however, lies in their failure to respect Congress's budget constraint—the very scarce time available for careful debate and decision-making. Congress cannot enact into law the entire Code of Federal Regulations. The piecemeal substitution of congressional for bureaucratic judgments—whether through rulewriting by the Congress itself or through the chipping away at the regulatory edifice by withdrawing agency jurisdiction on a case-by-case basis—does not respond to the need for a *process* that would require decision-makers to make tradeoffs between various regulatory objectives and to make midcourse corrections as new data arrive. In short, statutory amendments to particular regulatory charters should be justified on their own merits and be limited to those cases of great importance or urgency. Such amendments should not be advocated as part of a broader strategy to cure the fundamental defects plaguing the regulatory process.

A different set of problems is raised by the other frequently discussed method of correcting the overdelegation problem: the congressional or legislative veto. Under this mechanism, Congress would grant itself the authority to veto final regulations before they take effect. In fact, Congress has enacted over 200 veto provisions in a wide array of areas, including educational assistance, foreign aid, energy policy, agriculture, trade agreements, and arms control.[6] Most recently, Congress has sub-

---

5. FTC Improvements Act of 1980 P.L.96–252. In 1982, the House (but not the Senate) approved an authorization bill that would have barred the FTC from investigating cases involving advertising, agricultural cooperatives, and state licensed professions, such as lawyers, doctors, and dentists.

6. Consumer Energy Council of America v. FERC, 673 F.2d at 453, n. 118. See also Congressional Reference Service, Library of Congress, "Congressional Review, Deferral, and Disapproval of Executive Action: A Summary and an Inventory of Statutory Authority," April 30, 1976 and "1976–77 Congressional Acts Authorizing Prior Review, Approval, or Disapproval of Proposed Executive Actions," May 25, 1978. For general discussions of the historical, legal, and political issues raised by the veto, see Harold H. Bruff and

jected all substantive FTC rules to a two-house veto process.[7]
The proponents of the veto as a method of checking agency power would go further, however, by establishing a generic veto provision applicable to the rules of *all* agencies. This idea appears to have been first advanced in the 94th Congress but attracted more attention in the following Congress with the introduction of H.R. 959, offered by Rep. Levitas (D-Ga.). Other veto proposals, of varying scope, were introduced at or around the same time, but received less publicity than the Levitas bill.[8] Some version of the veto was also included in several of the comprehensive regulatory reform proposals introduced in the 97th Congress, as described later in this chapter. In particular, a two-house veto provision was included in S. 1080, the omnibus regulatory reform package passed unanimously by the Senate in March 1982 (discussed below). The fear that a similar provision would be attached to the House bill was one of the reasons that the House leadership dragged its feet in bringing the corresponding omnibus reform bill to a floor vote in the House. This fear notwithstanding, the proposed regulatory reform legislation reported to the House floor in fact included a legislative veto clause.

The generic legislative veto proposals have several common features. Newly promulgated rules would generally not become effective if (1) within a certain period, such as 90 or 120 days of continuous congressional session, one or both houses adopted by majority vote a resolution of disapproval, or (2)

Ernest Gellhorn, "Congressional Control of Administrative Regulation: A Study of Legislative Vetoes," *Harvard Law Review,* May 1977, pp. 1369–1440; Carl McGowan, "Congress, Court, and Control of Delegated Power," *Columbia Law Review,* December 1977, pp. 1119–74.

7. FTC Improvements Act of 1980.

8. Thus, veto provisions were attached to Hatch Act reforms, pesticide registration legislation, HUD authorization legislation, and the bill creating the Department of Energy but in each case did not survive deliberations by the conference committees. The Carter administration was able to thwart a congressional initiative to attach a legislative veto to legislation enabling the President to impose oil import quotas. The final compromise permitted congressional vetoes that may themselves be vetoed by the President.

within a certain period, one house adopted a resolution of disapproval that was not overturned by the other house. Emergency regulations would not be subject to the veto procedure, but could remain in effect only for a limited period. The original Levitas bill explicitly provided that the failure of Congress to veto a rule would not affect the private rights of individuals to challenge it in court. Finally, some of the legislative veto proposals limit the veto procedure to a trial period (e.g., four years).

One of the major difficulties with the use of the legislative veto, in either its specific or generic form, as a method of regulatory reform, however, is its questionable constitutionality. In January 1982, the United States Court of Appeals for the District of Columbia issued a broad holding in *Consumer Energy Council of America v. FERC,* striking down the constitutionality of the veto as applied to regulatory decisions.[9] At issue in *Consumer Energy Council* were regulations promulgated by FERC (the Federal Energy Regulatory Commission) to implement the "incremental pricing" program established by the National Gas Policy Act of 1978 (NGPA), a program designed to shift part of the price increase resulting from the deregulation of "new" natural gas from residential to industrial gas users. The Phase II incremental pricing regulations were issued by FERC in May 1980, but were disapproved two weeks later by the House under a provision of the NGPA allowing the regulations to be vetoed by either house within thirty days of issuance.

The House action provided a clear test of the constitution-

9. Two earlier court decisions had split on the constitutional issue in a non-regulatory context. In Atkins v. United States, 556 F.2d 1028 (Ct. Cl. 1977) (per curiam), *cert. denied,* 434 U.S. 1009 (1978), the Court of Claims upheld the one-house veto provision of the Federal Salary Act, under which the President's recommendations for salaries of certain government officials become legally effective unless either house of Congress disapproves within thirty days. Conversely, in Chadha v. Immigration and Naturalization Service, 634 F.2d 408 (1980), the Court of Appeals for the Ninth Circuit struck down the constitutionality of a provision of the Immigration and Nationality Act allowing either house to veto a suspension of deportation granted by the attorney general. The Supreme Court heard argument on the latter case and the *Consumer Energy Council* decision in December 1982.

ality of the veto. Constitutional critics had charged that the congressional veto process prevented the President from exercising his own constitutionally authorized veto power.[10] In addition, critics had argued that the veto violated the hallowed principle of separation of powers implicit in the Constitution, because it permitted Congress to share powers properly exercised by the executive and judicial branches. Advocates of the veto, on the other hand, had defended its constitutionality by contending that the veto represented a legitimate means by which Congress could limit its delegation when first passing legislation.

The D.C. Circuit came down squarely on the side of the critics. It concluded that the veto violated both the presidential veto provisions of Article I, Section 7, and the separation of powers principle. The court summed up its holding this way:

> The fundamental problem of the one-house veto, then, is that it represents an attempt by Congress to retain direct control over delegated administrative power. Congress may provide detailed rules of conduct to be administered without discretion by administrative officers, or it may provide broad policy guidance and leave the details to be filled in by administrative officers exercising substantial discretion. It may not, however, insert one of its houses as an effective administrative decision-maker.[11]

The *Consumer Energy Council* decision was joined nine months later in *Consumers Union v. FTC,* 1982–83 Trade Cas. ¶ 64,994 (D.C. Cir. 1982), when the D.C. Circuit struck down the congressional veto of the FTC's controversial rule governing

10. Article I, Section 7, Clause 2 provides that "Every Bill which shall have passed the House of Representatives and the Senate, shall, before it becomes a Law, be presented to the President of the United States." Clause 3 of the same section provides that "Every Order, Resolution, or Vote, to which the concurrence of the Senate and House of Representatives may be necessary (except on a question of Adjournment) shall be presented to the President of the United States."

11. Consumer Energy Council of America v. FERC, 673 F.2d at 476. The Court made clear elsewhere in its opinion that it felt the same way about two-house veto provisions.

disclosure by used car dealers (the "used car" rule). Both decisions have been appealed to the Supreme Court, which is expected to issue a final decision on *Consumer Energy Council* and the other legislative veto case before it, *Chadha v. Immigration and Naturalization Service,* in Spring 1983. While it is difficult to predict the outcome of a Supreme Court ruling in this area, there is little question that the D.C. Circuit's opinions have cast a long shadow on the constitutionality of the veto as a means for reining in the delegated power of the administrative agencies.

Even if it were constitutional, however, the veto process is a poor mechanism for remedying those defects in the current regulatory process that we believe to be of central importance. Like the proposals to amend individual regulatory charters, the legislative veto introduces Congress into the regulatory decision-making arena on a sporadic basis. True, a veto process permits Congress to let off steam by blocking particularly controversial rules. But that is all it does. Unlike the presidential veto of an appropriations bill, which is generally exercised to further the larger objective of the President's program, the legislative veto of individual rules takes place in a vacuum. Since the veto mechanism provides no comprehensive perspective analogous to the expenditure budget, it does nothing to encourage individual congressmen, let alone Congress as a whole, to develop interest or expertise in making tradeoffs between regulatory objectives. Rather, because the veto allows Congress the choice of only affirming or nullifying a final agency rule promulgated after extensive rulemaking proceedings, the veto of any individual rule can easily be transformed into a symbolic referendum on the operation of the agency generally—or even of the President himself—rather than on the merits of any particular rule.

In sum, both sets of proposals to increase congressional involvement in the rulemaking process miss the heart of the current problem. Each will ultimately be used infrequently at a time when a broader structural framework is needed to confront decision-makers with tradeoffs between regulatory objectives. Each would involve only the Congress and exclude the Executive, whose coordinating function is needed to provide Congress with a comprehensive set of choices among a wide variety of regulatory alternatives—within and across regulatory programs and statutes. And neither suggestion would involve Congress in the rulemaking process in a way that would be most useful: in determining broad regulatory priorities among regulations and between regulation and other approaches to economic and social problems. Correcting specific statutory charters may be a worthwhile enterprise by itself, but it is extremely limited and still leaves the agencies substantial discretion to make rules thereafter without effective congressional supervision. The veto comes too late, well after the priority-setting stage and outside a structured framework that is needed to discipline regulatory decision-making.

2. Enhancing Presidential Authority

The recent regulatory reform report issued by the American Bar Association's Commission on Law and the Economy has addressed the political accountability problem from a somewhat different direction.[12] The commission points to many of the same problems with the current regulatory process identified here, including the need for a mechanism to balance diverse national goals and policies. But unlike the advocates of the legislative veto, who have urged that the Congress take the lead in any suggested procedure for addressing these problems, the commission expresses the view that the *President* should be at the heart of that process. Individual agencies have single missions to pursue; so, often, do Congressmen. Since only the President is responsible to a *national* constituency, the commission recommends that a mechanism be established to resolve conflict among regulatory objectives and that the President —through his Executive Office—assume precisely that role.[13]

The President's authority, however, is circumscribed by

12. *Federal Regulation: Roads to Reform* (Washington, D.C.: American Bar Association, 1980). (Hereinafter cited as *Federal Regulation*.)

13. The same argument is made in an earlier article by Lloyd N. Cutler and David R. Johnson which the commission acknowledges to be its source for the proposal described in this section. See Lloyd N. Cutler and David R. Johnson, "Regulations and the Political Process," 84 *Yale Law Journal* 1395 (1975).

the Constitution. In the case of the independent agencies, the President clearly lacks the authority, in the absence of explicit statutory direction, to direct the outcome of a regulatory decision. The ABA commission asserts that the same may also be true in the case of executive branch agencies, although recent case law would appear to give the President broad authority in this area.[14]

To remedy the problem, the commission has urged the adoption of a "report and wait" procedure under which the regulations of independent and executive agencies would take effect automatically after certain periods of time unless Congress passed *legislation* to the contrary. Because the legislation may be vetoed by the President, report and wait provisions are clearly constitutional, differing sharply from legislative vetoes, which are not subject to presidential veto.

The "report and wait" procedure recommended by the ABA commission contains three essential features:

(1) a statutory grant of carefully limited presidential power to direct certain regulatory agencies to take up and decide critical regulatory issues within a specified time period, and to modify or reverse certain agency actions relating to such issues;

(2) an executive or statutory requirement that, before completing major actions, regulatory agencies prepare analyses and conduct interagency reviews under presidential auspices appraising the impact of the proposed action on all statutory goals; and

(3) an appropriate and constitutional opportunity for congressional review of each presidential exercise of the power of intervention proposed above, and of certain other presidential exercises of congressionally delegated authority.[15]

The first and third elements are the heart of the procedure. Under (1), the President could intervene in certain "critical" rulemakings within a certain period of time. His reasons for

14. The commission identifies six statutes that specifically grant the President the right to review and approve decisions by both independent and executive branch agencies. See *Federal Regulation,* p. 100.

15. *Federal Regulation,* p. 101.

intervening would be explained in the *Federal Register*. Any
modifications in an agency's decision would have to be consistent with underlying statutory standards. Under (3), Congress
would have seventy days to modify the President's action by
statute. If no Congressional action were taken within the
seventy-day period, the President's modification would stand
(unless within the period the President had further amended or
withdrawn his action). The second feature (2)—requiring the
preparation of analyses of proposed rules—is either already
required by executive order or is included in the comprehensive
regulatory reform proposals discussed below. Procedures governing *ex parte* contacts would be the same for all government
parties—agencies, the President, and the White House staff.
Finally, the President's power to direct agency decisions would
apply, with exceptions, to both executive and independent
agency rulemakings; the exceptions would be the money market functions of the Federal Reserve Board, the campaign
financing functions of the Federal Election Commission, certain functions of the CAB and FCC, and "adjudications" in
which the right to a specific right or privilege may be contested.

Whatever position one may take as to the merits of the
ABA proposal, it is an exceedingly modest step. Indeed, with
one exception,[16] it does not even make a material change in
existing law. Since the "report and wait" mechanism permits
Congress to modify agency action only by passing legislation,
the procedure does nothing more than institutionalize a formal
schedule for the exercise of normal congressional powers. The
proposal adds little to presidential powers as well. Both the
Carter and Reagan administrations have strongly backed—and
the courts have upheld—the President's constitutional right to
direct the nonadjudicative decisions of executive branch regulatory agencies, even when authority to make such decisions

16. The only extension of existing authority under the commission proposal is the ability it would give the President, under provision (1), to overrule
independent agency quasi-legislative rules. As we noted above, however, such
rules are relatively scarce—most independent agency rulings apply to specific
parties—so this extension of authority would be quite limited.

has been delegated by the Congress to inferior executive officials. In practice, it is difficult to conceive that a President, who has the authority to hire and fire his cabinet officers, may not influence the outcomes of important regulatory decisions that must be made by executive branch agencies.[17] As the Court of Appeals for the District of Columbia held in its decision sustaining the EPA's sulfur scrubbing rule against legal challenge:

> The authority of the President to control and supervise executive policymaking is derived from the Constitution; the desirability of such control is demonstrable from the practical realities of administrative rulemaking. Regulations such as those involved here demand a careful weighing of cost, environmental, and energy considerations. They also have implications for national economic policy. *Our form of government simply could not function effectively or rationally if key executive policymakers were isolated from each other and from the Chief Executive. Single mission agencies do not always have the answers to complex regulatory problems. An overworked administrator exposed on a 24-hour basis to a dedicated but zealous staff needs to know the arguments and ideas of policymakers in other agencies as well as in the White House* [emphasis added].[18]

President Reagan's Executive Order 12291 has already institutionalized Executive Office oversight, at least with respect to the executive branch agencies. It is possible that any omnibus regulatory reform package approved by Congress would extend Executive Office oversight to the independent agencies as well. Under these circumstances, the spirit, if not

17. During the Carter administration, the Department of Justice affirmed the right of the President's advisers, particularly the Council of Economic Advisers, to discuss issues related to the Interior Department's proposed strip mining rules after the public comment period had closed but prior to the issuance of the final rule. In the course of this opinion, the department affirmed the constitutional authority of the President over subordinate officials in the executive branch. "Memorandum for Cecil Andrus," Opinion of the Assistant Attorney General, Office of Legal Counsel, Department of Justice, January 1979.

18. Sierra Club v. Costle, 657 F.2d 298, 406 (D.C. Cir. 1981).

the letter, of the ABA's recommendation of strong presidential oversight is well on the way toward being fully accomplished. These remarks should not be taken as an indication of skepticism about executive branch regulatory oversight. Ultimately, any effective and coherent program must be directed by the presidential staff—and under the Reagan administration this approach has begun to take root. But strong presidential oversight alone will not meet the need for elected officials in *both* political branches of the federal government to make regulatory decisions in a broad context that requires tradeoffs to be made between regulatory programs. Thus even where a presidential or congressional action on an individual rule is grounded in a careful, thorough analysis of all relevant costs and benefits, both branches still lack an overall perspective of competing regulatory objectives and the economic impacts of regulatory action. Neither the report and wait mechanism recommended by the ABA nor the legislative veto would provide that perspective, which is key to correcting both the political and economic defects pervading the current process.

3. *Relying on the Courts*
Both the legislative veto and the ABA commission proposal have been put forth as means of restoring greater *political accountability* to the regulatory process. Senator Dale Bumpers of Arkansas has suggested that the delegation problem be confronted instead by enhancing the power and responsibility of the *courts* to review agency decisions.

The vehicle for implementing this suggestion has come to be known as the "Bumpers amendment." Under its original version, which passed the Senate in 1980 as an amendment to the Federal Courts Improvement Act, agencies would be required to meet much stiffer tests than the existing "arbitrary and capricious" or "substantial evidence" standards before the courts would be authorized to uphold their rules. Specifically, reviewing courts would be directed to uphold challenged regulations only if the agencies could support the factual underpinnings of their rules by a "preponderance of the evidence." In addition, the amendment would require courts to judge legal issues independently and not to defer to prior agency practice or "expertise."

Despite its popularity in the Senate, the version of the Bumpers amendment just described was opposed by both the Carter and Reagan administrations as well as by some thoughtful judicial observers.[19] Why should judges, whose primary expertise lies in reviewing agency compliance with procedural requirements, be any better at deciding substantive regulatory issues than knowledgeable experts in the agencies? Moreover, stronger standards of judicial review could very well encourage the filing of additional legal challenges to agency decisions, placing further strain on a judicial system already overburdened. The skepticism of the Reagan administration was particularly ironic: although many political conservatives had earlier been sympathetic to higher legal standards of review for regulations, they realized that during the Reagan period any new legal hurdles would only frustrate efforts to roll back rules already on the books.[20]

Such criticisms have blunted but not thwarted Senate support for a Bumpers-like provision. As we discuss further below, in March 1982 the Senate passed an omnibus regulatory reform package containing a revised version of the Bumpers amendment that no longer included the "preponderance of evidence" test for factual determinations. Instead, the legislation required that in determining whether a particular rule was "arbitrary or capricious," a reviewing court must ascertain whether the factual basis of a rule has "substantial support." In addition, the bill included the provision in the original version specifying that courts "independently" decide all questions of law.

It is questionable whether either of these modifications change present law in a material way. Spelling out that agency rules have "substantial support" is not much different from

19. J. Skelly Wright, "Should Judges Be Meddling Less in Running the U.S.?" *Harvard Civil Rights and Civil Liberties Law Review,* Spring 1980, pp. 1–28.

20. See Antonin Scalia, "Regulatory Reform—the Game Has Changed," *Regulation.* January/February 1981, pp. 13–15.

requiring agencies to show that the rules are supported by "substantial evidence," a requirement already applicable to many agency rules.[21] Adding the word "independently" to a reviewing court's obligations to decide legal issues also produces very little change, since the Administrative Procedure Act already requires that reviewing courts "shall decide all relevant questions of law."[22] The purpose of both modifications would thus appear to be more hortatory than substantive, signaling to the courts a strong congressional intent that they at least take a "hard look" when reviewing agency rules.[23]

Even if a similar or even stronger version of the Bumpers amendment is passed in the House, it should be clear that more active participation by *courts* in reviewing agency rules would do nothing to address the fundamental *political* problems with the regulatory process we have identified. The courts can do nothing to alter restrictive statutory mandates. Nor are they permitted (nor should they be) to compare and trade off the effectiveness of diverse regulatory efforts. The Bumpers amendment should thus be recognized as an attempt to pass the buck for addressing the problems that have surfaced with the regulatory process to the courts—without charging both *political* branches of the federal government to take greater responsibility for the manner in which society's resources are allocated through regulatory decisions.

The great irony, however, arises in the inconsistency of the

21. Traditionally, the "arbitrary and capricious" standard of judicial review has been applicable only to rules developed through informal rulemaking procedures and the "substantial evidence" standard to rules developed through formal rulemakings. This distinction has broken down, however, to the point where some reviewing courts generally consider the tests to be equivalent. *See, e.g.*, Pacific Legal Foundation v. Department of Transportation, 593 F.2d 1338, 1343 at n. 35.

22. 5 U.S.C. §706.

23. Often, the "mood" of Congress can be more important than the actual language of the statute. *See* Universal Camera Corp. v. NLRB, 340 U.S. 474, 487 (1951) (Frankfurter, J.).

Bumpers approach with the widespread aversion to judicial activism. Just as one group of senators is attempting to strip from the courts the authority to rule on such diverse subjects as busing or abortion, another equally conservative group would encourage greater activism in reviewing any regulations written to implement the wide variety of regulatory statutes.

Addressing the Inefficiency of Individual Rules

As we highlighted in chapter 4, the current regulatory process suffers not only from insufficient political attention but also from inefficiency. A primary reason for this second shortcoming is that neither political branch of the government currently compares the costs and benefits of *different* regulatory programs with a view toward channeling national resources to those areas where the potential social benefits per dollar expended are the greatest.

Moreover, neither branch of government now pays attention to what we label in the following discussion "macro-allocational" issues—those involved when one looks across both regulatory and expenditure programs. None of the regulatory reform proposals in the public arena proposes to address this aspect of regulatory inefficiency. Rather, as we discussed in chapter 3, the progress that is being recorded is concentrated at the program (or micro-allocational) level—improving the effectiveness of *individual* rules through requirements that agencies thoroughly analyze the consequences of regulatory proposals before putting them into effect. Such procedural measures have been instituted in the hope that better analysis will, subject to certain statutory restrictions, lead eventually to rules that are both cost-beneficial and designed in the most cost-effective manner available.

The attempt to improve analysis has been at the heart of recent congressional efforts to pass omnibus regulatory reform legislation. The Carter administration made a strong effort to convince Congress to pass its proposal (S.755), which essentially would have enacted Carter's Executive Order 12044 into law and extended its regulatory analysis requirements to the independent agencies. Similar bills, proposed during the Carter administration by Senators Ribicoff (S. 262) and Culver (S. 2147), would have charged a central agency—the OMB, the Comptroller General, or a new Regulatory Policy Board—with responsibilities for overseeing agency compliance with the analysis requirements. On the House side, Representatives Rodino and Danielson introduced H.R. 3263, which tracked its Senate counterpart in mandating that regulatory analyses be performed for "major" rules but was amended in committee also to contain a modified Bumpers provision and a two-house legislative veto procedure.[24]

The prospects for passage of some type of regulatory reform package improved when President Reagan assumed office in 1981. The President had made regulatory reform a major campaign theme. Moreover, the President's friend and ally, Senator Laxalt, was backing omnibus legislation (S. 1080), as was Rep. Danielson (H.R. 746), chairman of the House Judiciary subcommittee that had considered regulatory reform legislation during the previous congressional session.

After consideration by both the Senate Judiciary and Government Affairs Committees, the full Senate passed S. 1080, with some important modifications, in March 1982. S. 1080 shared the major features of earlier bills: it codified the regulatory analysis requirement—the latest version set forth in Reagan Executive Order 12291—and extended that requirement to the independent agencies.[25] The major innovation in S.

24. For a more detailed description of the legislative activity in this area during the Carter administration, see *Major Regulatory Initiatives During 1980* (Washington, D.C.: American Enterprise Institute, 1981). Congress did pass two regulatory initiatives in the Carter years, "The Paperwork Reduction Act of 1980" and "The Regulatory Flexibility Act." Under the first act, the OMB is given broad authority to oversee federal government information policies, with a view toward reducing the "paperwork burden" imposed by federal agencies on the private sector. The second act requires each federal agency to submit a "regulatory flexibility analysis" projecting the potential consequences of regulatory proposals for small business.

25. The bill incorporates the concept that has been present in three successive executive orders on regulation of limiting the analysis requirements only to

1080 is that it would institutionalize the broad oversight role accorded to the OMB by the Reagan executive order. Thus, not only would the OMB have the authority to oversee the rulemaking activities of *both* the executive branch and independent regulatory agencies, but the bill would explicitly authorize the OMB to exercise those powers to alter executive branch agency rulemaking proposals conferred by the Reagan executive order. The only restriction on the OMB provided under the Senate bill is that changes in proposed regulations resulting from OMB intervention would have to be noted in the agency's public rulemaking file.[26]

In December 1982, however, the regulatory reform proposal died in the House when it failed to survive a vote in the House Rules Committee. As of this writing, it is unclear whether the new Congress convening in 1983 will be able to muster a coalition to pass a new bill. One factor believed to have slowed the progress of the reform bill in 1982 was the lukewarm support received initially from the Reagan administration. The administration's reluctance was apparently due, at least in part, to the desire to avoid the creation of new legislative obstacles to its own executive reform initiatives. In addition, several voices

---

"major" rules. Specifically, the bill permits agencies or the President to determine whether a rule is "major" according to several criteria, including whether the rule is projected to have an annual economic effect of $100 million or more, to cause a "substantial" increase in prices, or to produce significant adverse effects on "competition, employment, investment, productivity, innovation, the environment, public health or safety," or the ability of U.S. companies to compete in international markets. Elsewhere, the bill provides that *Presidential* determinations of whether a rule is "major" are not judicially reviewable. Where an *agency* makes that determination, however, the bill permits judicial review but requires a "clear and convincing" showing of error before a determination that a rule is "major" can be overturned.

26. The Senate rejected a proposal made by Senator Levin that would have required the OMB to make public all of its contacts with both agency officials and outside parties. That such an amendment was considered by some senators to be necessary is perhaps an acknowledgment by at least those Senators that officials inside the Executive Office are not treated under current law in the same fashion as outside parties with respect to the rules prohibiting "ex parte" contacts.

in the administration expressed concern that any omnibus bill could include a legislative veto provision, which was viewed as an undesirable restriction on executive authority. Both of the administration's concerns were apparently sources of controversy between the House and Senate as well. Less controversial was the Bumpers provision, a version of which was included in both House and Senate bills. It remains to be seen whether these obstacles can be surmounted in the new Congress.

Putting the weakened Bumpers provision and a possible legislative veto clause to one side, it is difficult to quarrel with the major thrust of the omnibus bills: that by requiring agencies to analyze their regulatory proposals, and by authorizing the OMB to supervise that process, better and more efficient regulations will emerge. At best, however, such legislation represents only an incremental step toward the fundamental *systemwide* reform that is necessary. Moreover, again excepting a possible legislative veto provision, the "better analysis" approach to the reform of individual regulations and the accompanying oversight provided by the OMB casts no role for congressional participation in regulatory decision-making.

In short, nothing in the omnibus bills would establish a framework in which *either* political branch would be required to set priorities across the entire regulatory effort. The regulatory reform packages ensure that many individual regulatory trees would be more frequently pruned but provide for no one to plan for the forest.

Dismantling Regulatory Programs

A third category of measures that have recently been characterized as "regulatory reform" consists of steps simply intended to scale back the regulatory effort. The Reagan administration has made no secret that reducing regulation—or providing "regulatory relief"—is a major element of its overall economic recovery program. As President Reagan stated on June 13, 1981:

During the Presidential campaign, I promised quick and decisive action. Since taking office, I have made regulatory relief a top priority. It is one of the cornerstones of my economic recovery program.[27]

Consistent with this objective, one of the administration's first acts upon assuming office was to speed the Carter administration's program of decontrol of crude oil and petroleum products. In the end, the price deregulation did not lead to significant price increases, a result largely attributable to the soft world oil market caused by the recession. The administration has displayed less zeal in seeking the dismantling of other economic regulatory programs.[28] A particularly disturbing act of backsliding occurred when the administration endorsed legislation that would permit cartelization of the shipping industry by exempting it from most of the antitrust laws.[29]

The Reagan reforms in the area of social regulation, spearheaded by the cost-benefit requirements of Reagan Executive Order 12291, do not per se provide relief. The regulatory analysis requirements, as well as the principles of cost-benefit analysis, are neutral with respect to whether or not a particular rule is desirable. If a regulatory proposal promises benefits exceeding costs and is designed in the most cost-effective manner, then it should be implemented, even if it adds a "burden" of compliance for certain firms in the private sector.

Despite the executive order's apparent neutrality as to the

27. Statement by the President on Regulatory Relief (press release, June 13, 1981).

28. *See* Robert Crandall, "Has Reagan Dropped the Ball?" *Regulation*, September/October 1981, pp. 15–18. One exception to the loss of momentum in economic deregulation came in the Bus Deregulation Reform Act, enacted in August 1982. This act loosened some of the restrictions on entry and now places the burden of proof on protesters rather than applicants. The Department of Transportation is pressing for further changes; *see Regulation*, July/August 1982, pp. 6–8.

29. For an unintelligible defense of this legislation, see *Economic Report of the President, 1983*. This legislation was approved by a 350–33 majority in the House in September 1982, as well as by the Senate Commerce Committee. The full Senate approved similar legislation in February 1983 by a 64–33 margin.

costs and benefits of specific rules, the order has been used by the administration largely to curtail the scope of federal regulatory activity. More specifically, the administration's relief program has consisted of four principal elements:

A reexamination of existing rules with a primary emphasis toward providing regulatory relief;

A marked slowdown in the issuance of new major regulations;

Substantial relaxation of efforts to enforce existing rules; and

Significant cuts in the operating budgets of regulatory agencies.

The details of each of these elements are elaborated below.

REVIEW OF EXISTING RULES. That the Reagan administration would make the review of existing rules a major part of its regulatory relief effort was evident even before it assumed office. In a widely publicized memorandum addressed to the then president-elect, David Stockman (later to be OMB director) and Rep. Jack Kemp (R-NY) discussed "Regulatory Ventilation" as a means of "jolt[ing] business confidence and market psychology in a favorable direction." The authors stated that the "first and most urgent" component of regulatory ventilation was a "well-planned and orchestrated series of unilateral administrative actions to defer, revise, or rescind existing and pending regulations where clear legal authority exists."[30]

The new administration has since claimed considerable success in accomplishing this objective. In a fact sheet distributed on December 30, 1981, it announced that 2,715 of the 2,781 regulations that had been "received for review" had in fact been reviewed. Of those regulations reviewed, ninety-one were returned to or withdrawn by the agencies. Perhaps more interesting is that of the total 2,781 regulations received, only forty-three were classified as "major" (i.e., those that imposed costs of over $100 million per year). The fact sheet advertised the aggregate annual savings from its review to be close to $2 billion and the one-time investment savings to range between $2.8 and $4.8 billion.

In accord with its support of regulatory analysis, the

30. "Avoiding a GOP Economic Dunkirk," p. 20.

Reagan administration has justified the rescissions and modifications of existing rules on a cost-benefit basis. In some cases, however, such as the NHTSA's rescission of the passive restraint regulations, the agencies' cost-benefit determinations have been strongly and successfully contested.[31] In addition, the administration has made little effort to hide the fact that its reviews of some rules have been designed primarily to provide relief to a troubled industry. Thus, a significant number of the reviews have been concentrated on regulations affecting the automobile industry. In a statement entitled "Actions to Help the U.S. Auto Industry" (April 6, 1981), the administration proclaimed:

> The Presidential Task Force and the Executive branch regulatory agencies will give high priority to relief for the auto industry. These measures will result in considerable savings in capital costs to the industry and even greater savings to consumers.

The fact sheet then listed thirty-four specific EPA and NHTSA regulations affecting the automobile industry that were targeted for rescission or modification. This list included such significant regulations as the NHTSA's passive restraint standards and a

31. For a detailed economic analysis of the most important rescission, that on passive restraints or automatic seat belts, *see* William Nordhaus, "The Passive Restraint Papers," processed 1981. The passive restraint rescission was challenged in November 1981 in the United States Court of Appeals for the District of Columbia by a substantial portion of the insurance industry. On June 1, 1982, the Court of Appeals overturned the NHTSA's rescission in a harshly worded opinion and ordered the agency to produce a new justification of its rescission ruling or, failing that, to initiate a new rulemaking. State Farm Mutual Automobile Insurance Co., et al. v. Department of Transportation, et al., 680 F.2d 206 (D.C. Cir. 1982), *cert. granted,* 103 S. Ct. 340 (1982).

More recently, the EPA's new "bubble policy" for nonattainment areas (regions where ambient air quality standards have not been attained) was also struck down by the D.C. Court of Appeals. NRDC, Inc., et al. v. Anne Gorsuch, 685 F.2d 718 (D.C. Cir. 1982). Although the court's decision rested largely on statutory grounds, the court also noted that the EPA had failed to provide adequate support for its assertion that the previous policy, requiring the installation of best available control technology at each individual source of pollution, actually inhibited the development of control technology and thereby retarded efforts to improve air quality.

variety of EPA air pollution standards that have since been rescinded or altered.

The most recent description of the Reagan administration's policy on regulation is contained in *A Progress Report* of August 1982.[32] This document lists the major program changes during the first twenty months of the administration. Table 5.1 pre-

Table 5.1.   Summary of Regulatory Actions during the Reagan Administration, 1981–82

Category or Reform	Estimated Annualized Savings (millions of dollars)
Eased Compliance Standards	
Automobiles and Trucks	
Passive Restraints	1,080
Rims and Bumpers	740
Other	820
Agriculture, Processing	500
Handicapped, Building and Subways	600
Bilingual Education	400
Other	890
Reduced Paperwork	
Clean Water Act	1,000
Other	460
Elimination of Faulty Guidelines	530
Increased Flexibility	890
Total	7,910

SOURCE: Annualized savings in table 5.1 are calculated by using the Reagan administration estimates of one-time investment savings and annual savings from Presidential Task Force on Regulatory Relief, *Reagan Administration Achievements in Regulatory Relief, A Progress Report,* August 1982. One-time investment savings are annualized at a 15 percent cost of capital and then added to annual savings to give total estimated annualized savings.

These figures exclude the cost savings under "Salary Requirements," such as those under Davis-Bacon Act, which are here treated as transfer payments. In addition, when ranges are given in the original, the figures presented are the arithmetic averages of the extremes.

32. Presidential Task Force on Regulatory Relief, *Reagan Administration Achievements in Regulatory Relief, A Progress Report,* August 1982 (hereinafter cited as *A Progress Report*).

sents a summary of the cost savings due to regulatory actions taken and uses the administration's estimates. According to this source, total annualized savings in 1982 prices (equal to current costs plus 15 percent of investment outlays) totalled $8 billion. While there is probably some puffery in these estimates (particularly the last four numbers), they do indicate a substantial relief effort of the Reagan administration when compared with the efforts of earlier administrations.

The major regulatory changes during the first twenty months, along with cost saving estimates from *A Progress Report*, were: the rescission of the passive restraint ($1 billion annually), bumper ($300 million annually), and multipiece rim ($445 million annually) standards; relaxation of rules on mechanically deboned meat products ($500 million annually); revision of standards for the handicapped ($600 million annually); and easing standards for bilingual education ($400 million annually).

Finally, the administration appears to have expanded the effort launched by its predecessor to introduce more economic incentives into regulatory programs. Its first initiative, a new "bubble" policy for nonattainment areas issued by the EPA, however, was recently struck down by the U.S. Court of Appeals.[33] More recently, in November 1982, the agency established for the first time a system of trading lead permits among gasoline refineries as part of new final regulations requiring the phasing out of the average lead content of gasoline. In addition, as 1982 came to a close, EPA apparently still had under consideration a proposal for expanding the bubble policy already in place in the agency's air emissions program to cover water pollution control as well.

THE SLOWDOWN IN THE DEVELOPMENT OF NEW RULES. The second element of the Reagan administration's regulatory relief package is the marked slowdown in the issuance of new rules. The Stockman/Kemp memorandum to President-elect Reagan made clear that such a change in direction was the second element of its broader regulatory ventilation strategy, advancing a suggestion offered by Murray

33. See note 31 above.

Weidenbaum (later to be the CEA chairman) that a one-year moratorium be imposed on all new rulemakings.

The administration quickly implemented the spirit if not the letter of the Stockman/Kemp recommendation. On January 29, 1981, barely one week after assuming office, the President directed all executive branch agencies to postpone for sixty days the effective date of the so-called midnight regulations left by the Carter administration—or all rules then in final form but not yet made effective—and all rules proposed but not yet made final. Two months later, on March 25, Vice President Bush extended the regulatory freeze on thirty-five specific regulatory proposals and added a list of twenty-seven existing regulations that were scheduled for review.

By the end of the year, the administration was able to claim that the number of new major regulations issued in 1981 had been cut in half compared to the number issued the previous year. This decline was reflected in one of the administration's favorite yardsticks of success—the number of pages in the *Federal Register*—which the administration claimed had fallen by one-third during the first ten months of 1981 as compared to a similar period of the previous year,[34] and in the 50 percent decline for the whole year in the number of judicial challenges to agency decisions in the D.C. Circuit (where most challenges to regulatory decisions are brought). By August 1982, *A Progress Report* stated that the flow of new rules had been reduced by one-third.[35] In addition, no major new areas of federal regulation were opened up during the first two years of the administration, a fact often touted by administration officials as one of the administration's major achievements in the regulatory area.

34. "Fact Sheet: Year-End Summary of the Administration's Regulatory Relief Program," December 30, 1981, p. 2. The drop in the number of *all* regulations (including those not classified as major) was reported at 21 percent. *BNA Daily Report for Executives,* April 23, 1982, p. A–28.

35. Very few of the new rules or proposals promised a major economic impact. Among the exceptions were the chemical labeling proposal offered by OSHA (estimated to cost industry over $200 million per year) and the EPA's final landfill regulation addressing the problem of hazardous wastes (with an annual price tag of over $500 million).

RELAXED ENFORCEMENT. Regulations impose no costs and produce no benefits if they are not enforced and complied with. Thus, even if new regulations continued to be issued at the same rate—with the same potential impact as in previous years—relief could be provided through relaxation in enforcement.

There are signs that this method of providing relief—or "statutory impoundment"—has been a major element of the administration's overall relief package. The following trends in enforcement activities at various executive branch agencies have been apparent:[36]

At the NHTSA, the number of formal investigations into potential car defects had fallen from an annual rate of fifteen during the Carter administration to approximately five during the Reagan period.

At OSHA, the number of monthly inspections had fallen 17 percent between 1980 and 1981. The falloff in average monthly follow-up inspections was even greater—68 percent—while the number of serious citations issued dropped by 27 percent.[37]

At the Department of the Interior, a new policy has been adopted to cut back on enforcement actions involving the federal surface-mining laws, where the lawsuits "conflict with the secretary's goals of decreasing regulatory restraints on productivity."

USDA has downgraded its food-safety compliance program; processing plants are no longer reviewed and rated on their compliance with federal health and safety rules.

Perhaps the most public attention has been given the EPA's apparent relaxation of enforcement efforts, particularly those in the agency's hazardous waste program. The relaxation of enforcement generally at the agency is indicated by the drop in the number of enforcement actions referred to the Department of Justice for prosecution, from an average of 200 per year

36. *Washington Post,* November 15, 1981, at F1.
37. The current OSHA Administrator has rebutted the charges that enforcement has been relaxed at his agency by contending that enforcement activity had fallen in the first or "transition" year in each of the two previous administrations. *BNA Daily Report for Executives,* April 2, 1982, p. A–3.
38. *Washington Post,* November 15, 1981, at F2.

during the 1970–80 period, to just 30 as of November 1981.[38] Although by the end of 1981, the rate had increased to seventy-eight, this level was 69 percent below the 252 cases that had been referred in 1980.[39] As congressional criticism of the EPA's enforcement efforts mounted, the referral rate climbed to ninety-one cases in the first three quarters of 1982, a level still far below the 1980 level.[40]

This decline in enforcement activity is troublesome in two respects. First, it does not resolve the ultimate issues and may increase the uncertainty about regulatory programs: at some point, a more sympathetic administration will arrive to enforce the statutes. Second, this apparent inattention to enforcing the law can only help foster an increasingly casual attitude toward compliance with inconvenient statutes, an attitude that can only help accelerate the crumbling respect for the rule of law.

CUTBACKS IN AGENCY OPERATING BUDGETS. The final and perhaps the most publicized prong of the Reagan administration's regulatory relief program has been the effort to cut the operating budgets of both the executive branch and independent agencies. This effort has not been pursued in a vacuum, of course, since budget cuts in nondefense programs have been a major element of the administration's overall economic recovery package. Nevertheless, there is little doubt that the cuts made in regulatory programs, in particular, have been part of an independent effort to restrain the regulatory agencies from raising private sector compliance costs by issuing new major regulations or enforcing old ones.

Tables 5.2 through 5.5 present federal outlays for major regulatory programs since 1959. These tables display the com-

39. The relaxation in EPA's enforcement activities is especially evident at the regional level, where the number of cases referred to agency headquarters dropped from 313 in 1980 to sixty-six in 1981, a decline of 79 percent. *BNA Daily Report for Executives,* April 8, 1982, p. A–10. The EPA's associate administrator for enforcement, Robert Perry, responded to the criticism of the agency's enforcement effort in August 1982, alleging that since the enforcement office had been reorganized, "record numbers" of enforcement actions had been referred to the Justice Department for prosecution. *BNA Environment Reporter,* August 13, 1982, pp. 483–84.

40. *BNA Environment Reporter,* October 15, 1982, p. 807.

Table 5.2. Defense, Regulatory, and Other Outlays of the
Federal Government: Selected Years, 1959–1983
(Fiscal Years; millions of dollars)

	1959	1969	1979	1981	Proposed 1983
Selected Regulatory Outlays	176	579	2,965	$ 4,019	$ 3,389
National Defense Outlays	46,426	81,240	117,681	159,765	221,068
All Other Outlays	34,095	102,737	373,027	493,420	533,181
Total Outlays	80,697	184,556	493,673	657,204	757,638
As Percentages of Total Outlays					
Selected Regulatory	0.22	0.31	0.60	0.61	0.45
National Defense	57.5	44.0	23.8	24.3	29.2
Other	42.3	55.7	75.6	75.1	70.4

NOTE: Details may not add to totals due to rounding.
SOURCE: U.S. government budget, fiscal years 1961, 1971, 1981, 1983; table 5.3 below.

parative severity of the proposed cutbacks in regulatory agency operating budgets. Thus, the Reagan administration's proposed budget for fiscal year 1983 calls for $3,389 million in regulatory spending, compared to $4,019 in fiscal 1981. This 15 percent cutback compares to a 15 percent increase in the overall budget in nominal terms.

In real terms, the budget proposes a 26 percent decrease in regulatory expenditures. This cut compares with a nearly unchanged overall budget over the 1981–83 period, with real defense outlays rising and nonregulatory civilian outlays scheduled to fall by 6 percent.

The regulatory cutbacks are not evenly distributed across all agencies. A significant portion represents the winding down of several economic regulatory agencies whose mandates were

Table 5.3. Selected Regulatory Outlays by Function: Selected
Years 1959– 1983 (Fiscal Years; thousands
of dollars)

	1959	1969	1979	1981	Proposed 1983
Consumer Safety and Health	42,084	141,961	808,666	914,055	684,223
Job Safety and Working Conditions	23,212	92,105	475,973	595,596	608,418
Energy and the Environment	N/A	191,761	1,252,790	1,959,914	1,681,081
Other Regulation (generally economic)	110,892	153,400	427,417	549,750	415,273
Total Regulatory Outlays	176,188	579,227	2,964,846	4,019,315	3,388,995

NOTE: The functional totals displayed consist of outlays for the following
agencies and their functional predecessors:

Consumer Health and Safety: CPSC, FDA, Antitrust Division, Federal Railroad Administration (regulatory activities), NHTSA, Bureau of Alcohol,
Tobacco and Firearms, Federal Highway Safety Administration (motor
carrier safety), National Transportation Safety Board.

Job Safety and Working Conditions: Mine Safety Health Administration,
OSHA, EEOC, NLRB.

Energy and the Environment: Petroleum regulation enforcement activities
(in Department of Justice in proposed budget), Economic Regulatory
Administration, OSM, EPA (excluding construction grants and superfund
outlays), Consumer Protection and Environmental Health Service (air
pollution outlays), Water Pollution Administration (regulatory activities),
NRC.

Other Regulation: CAB, CFTC, FERC, FPC, FMC, FTC, ICC, SEC.

reduced by actions during the previous administration. For
example, reductions in energy regulation and at the CAB account for over $100 million of the $600 million cut in regulatory
spending. Better indications of the Reagan administration's
regulatory philosophy are the cuts at the National Highway
Traffic Safety Administration and the Environmental Protection Agency. The President has proposed cutting the NHTSA's
budget by a third, a savings of $93 million between 1981

Table 5.4. Defense, Regulatory, and Other Outlays in
Constant Dollars, Selected Years, 1959–1983
(Fiscal Years; millions of 1972 dollars)

	1959	1969	1979	1981	Proposed 1983
Selected Regulatory Outlays	261	667	1,821	2,076	1,530
National Defense Outlays	68,678	93,605	72,299	82,532	99,805
All Other Outlays	50,436	118,374	229,174	254,892	240,714
Total	119,375	212,647	303,294	339,500	342,049

SOURCES: Current dollar figures are taken from table 5.2 above. These are
converted to constant dollars using the GNP deflator from *Economic Report of
the President, 1982*

Table 5.5. Selected Regulatory Outlays by Function in
Constant (1972 = 100) dollars, Selected Years,
1959–1983 (Fiscal Years; thousands of 1972
dollars)

	1959	1969	1979	1981	Proposed 1983
Consumer Safety and Health	62,254	163,568	496,815	472,185	308,904
Job Safety and Working Conditions	34,337	106,124	292,421	307,674	274,681
Energy and the Environment	N/A	220,948	769,669	1,012,457	758,953
Other Regulation (generally economic)	164,041	176,748	262,590	283,991	187,482
Total	260,632	667,389	1,821,495	2,076,307	1,530,020

SOURCE: Table 5.3; deflated as described in table 5.4 above.

and 1983. This agency has been in the forefront of the administration's effort to modify or rescind existing rules as well. The EPA's operating budget (which excludes nonregulatory activities) would drop 21 percent between 1981 and 1983, were the President's budget to be approved. Even this figure—a $281 million drop—masks a highly controversial cutback in research funds at the agency, which the Reagan administration has proposed to cut from $247 million to $166 million between fiscal 1981 and 1983—a 33 percent decline. This decline in research and development is hard to rationalize in light of the administration's commitment to thorough analysis of both the costs and benefits of regulatory proposals.

What is the overall scorecard on the Reagan administration's program of regulatory relief after two years? Is the Reagan approach—resembling a Ralph Nader movie run in reverse—a useful model for the future?

The record is clearly quite mixed. The most important step has been the establishment of high-level central executive branch review, analysis, and decision-making in the OMB. The need for such authority has been recognized for some time (it was proposed in October 1978 but was washed overboard by a wave of regulators' indignation). While currently understaffed, the OMB unit—or something like it—will be the kernel for any future larger presidential oversight in the regulatory arena. In addition, the endorsement (in spirit if not in action) of weighing costs and benefits has laid the foundation for a more balanced approach to determining the proper stringency of rules.

Second, the substantive record on social regulations has been mixed. No major programs have been born; some old ones have been trimmed. The lack of enforcement and the budget cuts are particularly disturbing, however, for they open up a serious gap between what is illegal and what is enforceable.

Third, in the area of substantive economic regulation, the record is also mixed. After an early start in speeding the decontrol of oil prices, little has been accomplished. If anything, there has been regression at the ICC, which has slowed deregulation of trucking and railroads, and in the financial area, with the administration's reluctance to speed up decontrol of interest rates of the thrifts. While the latter has some economic justification due to the fear of the demise of the thrift institutions, the former appears to reflect mainly political favoritism.

Fourth, in the legislative arena, the administration has been surprisingly inactive. The most serious missed opportunity was its inability to shape a consensus on needed revisions to the Clean Air Act—a law filled with economic inefficiencies and anachronisms. Moreover, the administration has not taken the lead on any process or generic reforms, such as the ones discussed in the first two parts of this chapter or in the next two chapters. Viewed in the perspective of its entire program, it is clear that the Reagan administration chose to concentrate its legislative efforts on its tax and expenditure programs and to use its existing authority to trim back regulatory costs.

Whatever one may view as the merits or demerits of the Reagan relief effort, the measures just described as regulatory relief clearly do not respond to the need for an institutional mechanism for monitoring and allocating *private sector compliance expenditures* devoted to the pursuit of regulatory objectives. Although reductions in agency operating budgets may translate into reductions in costs incurred by the private sector, they affect both costs and benefits in a highly haphazard and undiscriminating fashion. The burden of regulatory review is also highly haphazard and fragmented—the bulk of it through 1982 providing relief to the auto industry.

Moreover, while portions of the Reagan program are beneficial, we believe there is a danger in clothing the probusiness program in the garb of neutral cost-benefit analysis. Such a course is certain to taint the worthwhile portions of the Reagan regulatory reform effort—to issue only cost-beneficial rules —with the more controversial desire by the administration to dismantle social regulatory programs and to reduce the scope of government. If a counter-reaction to the Reagan regulatory policies comes—and we suspect one will—there is a danger that the commitment to sound analysis and innovative regulatory tools will be washed overboard by a wave of regulatory zeal.

6

A Regulatory Budget

In the last chapter, we reviewed several current regulatory reform proposals and outlined their strengths and shortcomings. In this and the next chapter, we turn to two innovative reform suggestions, the regulatory budget and the legislated regulatory calendar. Conceptually, the regulatory budget is preferable, since it solves the two fundamental problems plaguing the current regulatory effort: inadequate political oversight and inefficiency. In practice, however, we think it is very unlikely that a regulatory budget could be implemented in the near future. Unlike federal expenditures, which are paid for directly by the Treasury, mandated private expenditures (MPEs) cannot be controlled directly by the government and are therefore difficult to monitor and audit. At present, this "funny money" problem, along with other major design issues, is sufficiently intractable to prevent the institution of any type of formal budget procedure for controlling regulation.

This does not mean that the regulatory budget should be ignored, however. As we suggested in chapter 4, the budget analogy is useful in highlighting the problems with the current regulatory effort. It should be equally helpful in designing solutions to those problems. In that sense, the *concept* of a regulatory budget may be viewed as an ideal type, within which a set of reforms can be molded. Understanding the ideal design may help sort out more limited, but also more practical, plans that may serve as a transition between the immediate and the ideal.

133

The discussion that follows is divided into two parts. In the first section, we outline the basic elements of a regulatory budget procedure and explain how it might work. We then discuss a series of specific problems that must be resolved before a budget procedure for regulation can be instituted.

Elements of a Regulatory Budget Procedure [1]

Given our discussion up to this point, the purpose of a regulatory budget cannot be a surprise. A budget would require legislators and administrators to make explicit decisions regarding the allocation of social resources both to regulatory goals generally and among specific regulatory programs in particular. Of central importance, a budgetary framework would change the way in which the regulatory effort is viewed. Individual regulatory programs would no longer be viewed in isolation, but rather would be compared—in terms of costs and benefits—against each other and against similar direct-expenditure programs.

To accomplish these objectives, the budget procedure must contain three key features: First, the budget must *impose dollar constraints* on mandated private expenditures. It is possible, of course, to conceive of other types of limits—numbers of pages in the Code of Federal Regulations (or *Federal Register*), numbers of "major" regulations, or hours of paperwork involved. While each of these alternative constraint measures may be easier to monitor, a budget procedure cannot be truly

1. We are aware of four previous efforts to discuss in some detail the concept of a regulatory budget: "The Regulatory Budget: Concepts and Information Requirements," in U.S. Department of Commerce, *Regulations Reform Seminar,* processed 1979; Christopher DeMuth, Richard H. Shackson, Eric O. Stork, and Arthur W. Wright, "The Regulatory Budget as a Management Tool for Reforming Regulation," a paper commissioned by the Joint Economic Committee, processed May 29, 1979; Julius W. Allen, "The Proposal for a Federal Regulatory Budget—An Overview," Congressional Research Service, JH2005 U.S. (September 12, 1979). For a legal analysis, see Lance D. Wood, Elliot P. Laws, and Barry Breen, "Restraining the Regulators: Legal Perspectives on a Regulatory Budget for Federal Agencies," *Harvard Journal on Legislation,* volume 18:1 (1981), pp. 1–33.

effective in producing the right kind of incentives unless it constrains total resource costs, i.e., dollars.

A second important feature is that the budget procedure *involve both the executive and legislative branches.* Under the federal expenditure model, the executive (through, say, the OMB) would propose a list of regulatory proposals together with budgeted private mandated expenditures (categorized either by agency or by program), which Congress would then authorize, subject to modifications. An essential element of the congressional review process, in turn, would be the creation of regulatory budget committees, charged with the task of sifting through the regulatory proposals and presenting a unified legislative package to the floor of each chamber. These committees would create a new set of congressional experts on the economics of regulation, just as the expenditure budget committees have created a class of congressmen with budgetary and general macroeconomic expertise. Of perhaps greater importance, the budget committees would create a group of representatives with vested interests in the larger overall consequences of government regulation to counteract the coalitions of narrow political concerns which each congressman and senator must also represent.

The third essential feature of the budget process is an effective *sanctions procedure.* In the case of federal expenditures, the sanction for exceeding budget limits is automatic: the Treasury refuses to authorize payment. There is no equally satisfactory counterpart for regulation. Private mandated expenditures are not controlled by the government. When an agency exceeds its mandated private expenditure budget ceiling, there is no automatic account that goes into the red; nor is it obvious what the government can and should do. As we discuss further below, it is this funny money problem, more than any other, that inhibits the implementation of a regulatory budget procedure at this time.

Although the detailed design of these three features will be discussed more fully below, the key elements are summarized in table 6.1, which compares an ideal regulatory budget procedure, modeled after its federal expenditure counterpart, with

Table 6.1. Steps in Current Regulatory Format and Under Ideal Regulatory Budget

Function	Current Regulatory Process	Regulatory Budget
I. *Legislative setting of broad policy goals*		
1. Purposes and techniques of regulation set by statute	✔	✔
2. Broad limits on authorization of mandated private expenditures ("regulatory authority") set by legislation		(✔)
II. *Executive initiation of regulation*		
1. Agency formulates a proposed regulation together with analysis of projected costs and benefits	✔	✔
2. Executive Office reviews major regulatory proposals and accompanying analyses	✔	✔
3. Executive Office, under direction from the President, makes choices between alternative regulatory proposals		✔
4. President submits regulatory budget to Congress. This budget contains "regulatory appropriations" and a calendar of major regulations:		✔
a. each regulatory agency has an overall limit		✔
b. major proposals are succinctly described, and have dollar ceiling		(✔)
III. *Legislative assent*		
1. Congress enacts the regulatory budget and authorizes agencies to issue Notices of Proposed Rulemaking (NPRM)		✔

Table 6.1. *(Continued)* Steps in Current Regulatory Format and Under Ideal Regulatory Budget

Function	Current Regulatory Process	Regulatory Budget
IV. *Final Regulation*		
1. Agency writes final proposal	✔	✔
2. Executive Office checks to make sure cost of major regulations and totals are within regulatory budget		✔
3. Final rule promulgated	✔	✔
V. *Audit*		
1. Subsequent to the promulgation of rules, some independent office (such as GAO) checks regulations to make sure costs are within authorized legislative ceilings		✔

NOTE: ✔ indicates this function performed under current regulatory process or regulatory budget.
(✔) indicates optional function under new regulatory budget.

the current regulatory process. The table depicts five stages, beginning with the enactment of legislation authorizing regulations to be issued, and ending with the auditing of final major rules to determine whether the private expenditures that have been mandated stay within the ceilings authorized by the regulatory budget. In contrast to the current process, which contains neither a "legislative assent" nor an "audit" stage, an ideal regulatory budget procedure would require decisions or action at all five stages.

The ideal regulatory budget may be illustrated by comparing how the development of an individual major regulation, say the EPA's rule requiring scrubbing of sulfur from the smoke produced at electricity generating plants, would be changed if a budget procedure were implemented. Under the current system, of course, agencies such as the EPA fill in the blanks of their statutory mandates by proposing rules, soliciting public comment, and then issuing rules in final form. Congressional input in this process is highly informal. If individual representatives have an interest in a rulemaking, they may either submit written (or oral) comments to the public docket or discuss their views informally with agency personnel.[2] In some cases, the relevant oversight and/or budget committee in Congress will later inquire about a particular rulemaking decision in the course of its annual review of agency activities. Except for those few regulatory activities subject to legislative vetoes, however, the rulemaking decisions of agencies will never be formally scrutinized by the Congress—either before or after the decisions are made.

A regulatory budget would change all that. Under the federal expenditure budget model, before a regulation such as the scrubber rule would even be proposed, it would be presented to a central clearinghouse within the executive branch—presumably the OMB—together with a preliminary analysis of its mandated costs and benefits. The OMB would compare the proposal with other proposals made by the same agency and other agencies and together with those agencies would work to compile and then to submit to Congress the government-wide

2. Where the latter course is followed, congressmen and senators must take great care to avoid pressuring agency officials to take factors into account other than those specifically mentioned in the legislation authorizing the regulatory proceeding. In D.C. Federation of Civil Associations v. Volpe, 459 F.2d 1231 (D.D. C. 1971), *cert. denied,* 405 U.S. 1030 (1972), the District of Columbia District Court remanded a decision by the Secretary of Transportation designating a proposed bridge as part of the interstate highway system on the grounds that the chairman of the House subcommittee with jurisdiction over the matter threatened publicly to withhold money for the District of Columbia subway system unless the bridge was approved by the Secretary. Even though the Court found no impropriety in the suggestion, it remanded the decision to ensure that the Secretary would make it solely on the basis of the factors included in the applicable authorizing statute.

In contrast, the Court of Appeals for the District of Columbia recently upheld the EPA's sulfur scrubbing rule in the face of a challenge based, in part, on the alleged impropriety of discussions between EPA officials and members of Congress after the public comment period on the rule had closed. Sierra Club v. Costle, 657 F.2d 298 (D.C. Cir. 1981). The court upheld the rule because it could find no evidence that the congressmen had urged the EPA to take account of factors other than those included in the Clean Air Act.

proposed regulatory budget. The deliberation by Congress on the proposed budget could be structured in various ways —some of which we will soon discuss. The essential feature of the regulatory budget process, however, would be the approval by the full Congress of both a total ceiling on all mandated private expenditures and individual ceilings broken down by agency or even by rule.[3] The final stage of the ideal budget procedure would be regular auditing and an effective sanctions mechanism for curtailing the regulation or disciplining the agencies in the event an authorized budget ceiling is exceeded.

In short, a regulatory budget procedure would involve both the Congress and a centralized office in the executive branch in agency rulemakings both before rules are proposed and after they are adopted. In the process, it would, at least in theory, restore political control over the regulatory process. We have argued up to this point that regulatory powers should be shifted from the selected to the elected, from agencies and courts to Congress and the President. This shift must, of course, take place in such a way that it takes advantage of the skills of each of the four groups. The skills of the President and Congress would be applied to choosing among general goals and balancing general costs and benefits. The budget procedure would create a structured and orderly environment in which these choices would be made and major regulatory issues routinely addressed.

A budget process for regulation would also make the pursuit of regulatory objectives more efficient by requiring regulatory decisions to emerge from the same two-level allocation mechanism, described in chapter 4, used by consumers and the government itself in authorizing public expenditures. On the aggregate level, a regulatory budget constraint would provide powerful incentives to Congress and the Executive to ensure that resources are allocated to the most important goals. If the threat from toxic substances appears greater, for example, then

3. The specific issues discussed here apply with equal force to the legislative regulatory calendar discussed in chapter 7.

that part of the "budget" can be increased; if escalating oil prices make environmental restrictions on coal more costly, such restrictions could be scaled back. At the agency or program-specific level, the budget procedure would enhance efficiency by encouraging regulators to transfer regulatory costs from low-yield to high-yield programs and to look around for more efficient regulatory techniques. Providing incentives for economizing to project managers is especially important, as they are likely to know better than anyone else the relevant tradeoffs and possible reforms.

The foregoing advantages of a regulatory budget remain theoretical of course, because, as we have already suggested, a formal budget procedure for regulation may be unworkable at the present time. In the next chapter, however, we will argue that a greater degree of political control over the regulatory process can be introduced without imposing a literal dollar constraint on mandated private expenditures. To foreshadow the issues that need to be addressed in designing such a control process, it is useful to explore in somewhat greater detail the problems that would have to be confronted if a formal budget procedure were to be established. The fact that some of these problems can be immediately resolved is what permits us to recommend a viable substitute for the regulatory budget in our concluding chapter.

Issues in Designing Regulatory Budgets or New Institutions for Regulatory Oversight

We have thus far only alluded to the three essential elements of a regulatory budget process: dollar constraints, congressional and executive branch participation, and an effective sanctions procedure. Exactly how each of these features would be designed, however, presents an entirely different set of questions for which there are no clear and ready answers. Without attempting to resolve each of them, we outline below what we believe to be the principal alternatives. The issues to which we turn have implications beyond the design of the regulatory budget, however, for many of them arise as well in the calendar proposal we discuss in chapter 7.

1. Scope of the Process

A first set of issues concerns the scope of the budget process. Specifically, should the budget apply to all regulatory activities of the federal government, or should it be restricted in some fashion? If some restrictions are appropriate, on what basis can they be justified?

Since the case for enhancing political control over the regulatory process rests, as we have suggested, on the political nature of regulatory decisions, we recommend that the budget process include those regulatory actions that are political (quasi-legislative) in nature.[4] The political element of regulatory decision-making is most evident where agencies have been given the quasi-legislative function of filling in the blanks of broad statutory authorizations—e.g., setting standards on emissions, announcing generic rules regarding entry into particular lines of business, allocating money from the superfund, and setting rules governing working conditions. When taking any of these actions, agencies are, in fact, performing a legislative function that has been delegated by the Congress. In contrast, such quasi-judicial tasks as investigation, planning, and enforcement—as well as such narrow decisions as who shall obtain a particular license or be eligible for a specific fare—are, by definition, more executive or judicial than legislative in nature and are thus reasonably excluded from a budget proposal.

The restriction of the regulatory budget to quasi-legislative, regulatory activities could be accomplished in two different ways. One alternative would be to write into the legislation authorizing the creation of the budget process those activities to be included. For example, the underlying legislation could expressly limit the budget procedure only to agency rulemakings and then only those rulemakings that do not involve the setting of rates or the granting of valuable privileges such as licenses.[5] This approach could be accomplished by

4. See chapter 3 for a discussion of the related issues in distinguishing between formal and informal rulemaking procedures.

5. The proposed omnibus regulatory reform legislation discussed in chapter 5 provides a model for this type of distinction. Thus, section 621(2) of H.R. 746 exempts from its requirements those rules:

excluding certain agencies—such as the ICC and the CAB —from the budget entirely on the grounds that they engage in very little regulatory activity of the type most suitable for inclusion in the budget.

The alternative approach would be to leave some discretion to the agencies to determine which rulemaking activities they prefer to be subject to the budget process. Thus, the legislation creating the budget procedure could simply specify that the budget process is to apply only to "rulemakings" rather than "adjudications"—as those terms are defined in the Administrative Procedure Act. This distinction would ensure that only those rulemakings of a strongly judicial character would be excluded from the budget process. At the same time, however, because agencies generally are permitted by their statutory mandates to choose between making rules by informal or formal procedures, an open-ended distinction between "rulemakings" and "adjudications" could permit the agencies to circumvent the budget process simply by changing the way in which they regulate.[6] Thus, it seems preferable, at the cost of some inflexibility, to set forth in the underlying legislation creating the budget procedure exactly what types of rulemakings (classified, perhaps, by the legislation that authorized those rulemakings) are meant to be covered by the budget process.

A second matter in defining the scope of the regulatory budget is to determine whether the budget would be limited solely to new regulations or whether all existing regulatory activity would have to be reauthorized annually. The answer to

---

(A) . . . involving the internal revenue laws of the United States; and

(B) . . . of particular applicability relating to rates, wages, corporate or financial structures or reorganizations thereof, prices, facilities, appliances, services, or allowances therefore, or to valuations, costs or accounting, or practices relating to such rates, wages, structures, prices, appliances, services or allowances.

6. There is evidence that at least some agencies have already begun to use formal rulemaking procedures more frequently in an effort to avoid the new analytical requirements applicable to informal rules. *See* Antonin Scalia, "Back to Basics: Making Law Without Making Rules," *Regulation,* July/August 1981, pp. 25–28.

this issue is an easy one, for it would be completely impractical to require annual reauthorization of the private expenditures mandated by all regulations. Moreover, budgeting all private mandated expenditures would pose an enormous burden on the sanctions procedure, under which compliance costs would have to be audited periodically. Finally, a procedure limiting coverage to new rules would be consistent with our ex ante accounting system proposed below. The most sensible course, therefore, would be to restrict the budget procedure to new regulatory proposals and to rely on a sunset procedure for reviewing the existing stock of regulatory actions on a five- or ten-year basis.[7]

A final issue regarding the scope of the process relates to the number of new proposals that should be subject to the annual budget procedure. The recent executive branch analysis requirements, for example, have applied only to major regulations, or primarily those projected to have an annual economic effect greater than $100 million. A similar cutoff is included in the proposed omnibus regulatory reform legislation now under consideration in Congress. The nation has some experience, therefore, with restricting a budget procedure to regulations having economic effects greater than $100 million. This cutoff could be varied in either direction, of course, depending on how ambitious Congress wanted to be in undertaking its regulatory reviews. Thus, a dollar level somewhat higher than $100 million—say $250 or $500 million—could be used initially and then later revised downward as Congress and the Executive obtained some experience with the number of regulatory proposals subject to the procedure.[8]

7. As a variation of relying solely on sunset to review existing rules, a budgetary credit or offset might be permitted for an early trade-in of old rules. Suppose that OSHA, as a typical example, were to decide its rule on toilet seats was unnecessarily burdensome and to abolish it. The agency might be permitted to credit 50 or 80 percent of the unused cost to other regulations. Such a "trade-in" rule would improve the (currently nonexistent) incentive of agencies to improve old rules.

8. To prevent agencies and the Executive from circumventing the binding effect of any threshold by splitting their regulatory proposals into several

2. *The Dollar Constraints*

Thus far, we have spoken somewhat loosely about the essential feature of any budget procedure for regulation: the dollar limits that must be placed on private mandated expenditures. This subject deserves more detailed attention, however. Exactly what types of dollar limits would be set, and where would they appear? How detailed would they be? Is the budget forward looking or contemporaneous?

The nature of the dollar constraints is linked to the issue of whether the budget procedure should apply only to new regulatory proposals or, more broadly, to a running total of all rules. If the regulatory budget procedure were limited to new proposals, the dollar constraints would appear in the annual budget proposed by the Executive and approved by Congress and would control only the private expenditures to be mandated by those new proposals. A "cumulative" regulatory budget, on the other hand, could be implemented either through an annual regulatory procedure—analogous to the procedure just outlined for new proposals—or through dollar constraints expressed in the individual statutes authorizing regulatory activities. Under the latter "statutory authorization" alternative, for example, Congress could write into the Clean Air Act the proviso that the private expenditures mandated by all rules promulgated pursuant to that act total no more than, say, $50 billion. Similarly, the Occupational Safety and Health Act could contain a budgetary limit of $10 billion, the Food, Drug, and Cosmetic Act a limit of $5 billion, and so on. These individual statutory limits could either supplement or serve as a substitute for an annual budget

---

pieces, the legislation authorizing the creation of the budget procedure could permit Congress to join together one or more related regulatory proposals that would have a combined effect greater than the statutory dollar threshold. Such a provision would have to require agencies to submit lists of all of their proposals—whether projected to exceed or fall below the statutory threshold—to Congress for initial screening to determine whether any proposals not included in the proposed regulatory budget should be included. To prevent this screening process from adding substantial delay to the regulatory process, the legislation could require that the relevant congressional committees make their determinations within a certain time period (e.g., thirty days).

procedure. As we suggest in the following section, the annual regulatory budget and the statutory authorization procedure could be implemented in very different fashions, with different mixes of executive and congressional involvement.

However inclusive the regulatory budget process is designed to be, an important issue that must be confronted is the level of detail of the budgetary constraints. In the case of the annual regulatory budget, should the limits apply only on an agency level, or should they also be broken down by individual statute, by regulatory program, or even by specific regulatory proposals? Clearly, the less detailed the constraints, the greater the discretion that will be accorded to the agencies in trading off the private sector effects of various rules or portions of rules. On the other hand, fewer details mean reduced control by Congress over the spending of private resources. In practice, if Congress were ever to establish a budget procedure for regulation, it probably would not want to specify the budgetary limits at any level more detailed than expenditures mandated by broad regulatory programs. It is conceivable that as more experience were acquired with the budget, the dollar limits could be broken down further, perhaps according to individual proposals.

The question of timing is related. Unlike the current expenditure budget, the regulatory budget for a given year should be stated in terms of the incremental costs mandated by the rule over the *lifetime* of the rule. Thus the sulfur scrubbing rule would be budgeted for, say, $40 billion over its life of 1979–88, rather than budgeted only for one year at, say, $4 billion. The use of such an unconventional accounting rule as lifetime cost is required more as a *control* mechanism than as an *accounting* device. Regulators and politicians should be aware of total costs down the road of actions taken today in order to have both the incentives and the tools to economize on costs mandated by regulations.

The lifetime cost accounting convention also has a logic that relates to the question of including old regulations in the budget. Because regulations are excluded from the budget after the first year, there must be a device to assure that agencies do not backload the costs of regulation. The easiest way to assure that old regulations are controlled is to include lifetime costs. Eventually, after old regulations have been sunsetted and reissued, all regulations would be caught in the net of the budget.

One other way to shortcut some of the many issues that arise in accounting is the use of an *ex ante accounting convention*. Such an approach uses estimates rather than actual outlays in setting dollar limits and in calculating the budget and would work in the following fashion. At the time a regulation is proposed, its costs would be estimated in great detail (in fact, such estimates are now routine in Regulatory Impact Analyses). These cost estimates are ex ante in the sense that they are made before the fact, rather than by calculating the actual outlays. Depending on the economic consequences of the rule, cost estimates could be reviewed before an adjudicatory body, say, by an administrative law judge, who would hear the cost estimates of all the parties and render a final judgment as to the ex ante accounting cost of a major regulation.[9]

Once the ex ante accounting cost was settled, it would then form the basis of the cost for regulatory budget purposes. This figure would be entered into the budget, and congressional or executive assent would apply to the ex ante costs.

There are significant advantages and disadvantages to such an approach. The major advantage is that it would cut the Gordian knot of the funny money problem—representing an acknowledgment that regulatory costs cannot be accurately tracked and measured and that best estimates would serve instead. Such an approach would also solve the sanctions issue, for regulations would not be legal unless the ex ante costs were within the limits of the current regulatory budget. Note, as well, that this concept fits in well with the rest of the design suggested here: it applies only to new regulations; given the cost and delay, it would be sensible only for major regulations; and it would apply on a life cycle basis.

9. The ex ante approach is in practice used in many investment decisions. When new, indivisible, military-procurement authorizations are made, it is recognized that an overrun will, in fact, be accepted as long as it is not totally unreasonable. In these cases, the primary budget tool is the original cost estimate.

The disadvantages of the ex ante costing approach are not insignificant. The major shortcoming is that it would allow a considerable amount of accounting discretion, whereby the supervisors of the accountants could impose their political wills. The issues of accounting treatment include discount rates, assumptions about overruns, treatment of incremental cost and technological improvement in abatement technology, as well as a host of even more technical issues. The ex ante approach would, as well, create a new regulatory bureaucracy designed to estimate and litigate regulatory costs. And, finally, there is no assurance that the ex ante costs would turn out to be accurate.

While the disadvantages of the ex ante accounting convention are severe, it would appear to be the most practical way of implementing the regulatory budget.

3. Congressional and Executive Branch Involvement[10]

An even more important element of the regulatory budget than the dollar constraints it would impose on private mandated expenditures is the involvement it would require of both the executive and legislative branches in the resolution of the fundamental political issues raised by the regulation of private sector activity. The federal expenditure budget process offers a well-known model for structuring this involvement at the stage when regulatory proposals are authorized. The precedents are less well established regarding the nature of congressional and executive participation in the monitoring of compliance with the budget and the methods for imposing sanctions.

The essential features of the current federal expenditure budget process are that the Executive proposes a budget that Congress then modifies and eventually approves. The key functions are performed by centralized bodies in both branches. In the Executive, the OMB performs the vital function of synthesizing the many budget requests of the various agencies and then compiling an overall budget recommendation by weigh-

---

10. Many of the issues discussed in this section apply equally to the legislated regulatory calendar discussed in chapter 7.

ing the merits of competing proposals. In addition, the other economic agencies within the executive branch—the Treasury Department and the Council of Economic Advisers—join with the OMB in using the budget process to propose a fiscal policy to achieve the reigning administration's macroeconomic objectives.

Similar functions are performed in Congress by the budget committees, which recommend overall budget ceilings to the full Congress. By passing a Concurrent Budget Resolution (usually in the month before the beginning of the fiscal year but more recently in the spring prior to the fiscal year), Congress sets budget ceilings that constrain the total expenditures that may be appropriated.

As we have already noted, the federal expenditure budget process is far from perfect, and in years when political consensus has broken down there are constant questions about its longevity. Nevertheless, it contains some important features that serve as good models for a regulatory budget. The concentration of budget responsibility and authority in centralized bodies in both branches draws power away from the individual agencies or congressional committees and the parochial interests they represent. In addition, something like the reconciliation process is essential to force decision-makers to recognize that resources are limited and should be allocated first to the highest priority programs.

Using the federal expenditure budget as a model, therefore, the two critical elements of any regulatory budget would appear to be (1) the creation of centralized bodies charged with regulatory budget responsibilities in both the executive and legislative branches and (2) some kind of procedure whereby the Congress can ensure that the total level of individual regulatory actions stays within an overall ceiling on private mandated expenditures. We have already discussed the first element by suggesting that the OMB serve as the centralized coordinator in the executive branch and that regulatory budget committees be created in each legislative chamber. The more difficult issue relates to the development of a satisfactory legislative reconciliation process.

One possible reconciliation procedure is to follow the federal expenditure budget model. Under this approach, the regulatory budget committees would first recommend to the full Congress a total ceiling on all private expenditures to be mandated by new regulatory proposals. After a ceiling were agreed upon, the individual committees charged with oversight of the various agencies could each set ceilings for those regulatory activities under their own jurisdiction. For example, the committees charged with oversight of the EPA could recommend a limit on private mandated expenditures of $10 billion, the OSHA oversight committee could recommend a ceiling of $5 billion, and so on. The regulatory budget committees would then perform the same reconciling function that the expenditure budget committees now perform for the appropriations process. Finally, Congress would approve the recommendations of the individual committees so long as the totals approved did not violate the overall regulatory resolution.

An alternative, and perhaps simpler, procedure would be to vest *both* the "budgetary" and the "appropriations" functions in the budget committees. Thus, the regulatory budget committees could first recommend a total regulatory budget ceiling to the full Congress and then also proceed to allocate mandated regulation expenditures within that total among the various regulatory programs, subject, of course, to full congressional approval. Alternatively, the regulatory budget committees could simultaneously prepare both the overall budget ceiling and the "appropriations" of regulatory expenditures for congressional consideration. Clearly, the vesting of such complete regulatory authority in the budget committees would have administrative advantages. On the other hand, it would represent such a significant transfer of authority and responsibility over regulatory affairs from the individual authorizing and oversight committees that it could very well be politically unacceptable to a majority of congressmen, who might otherwise be inclined to institute a regulatory budget procedure.

4. Sanctions and the "Funny Money" Problem
The problem of designing effective sanctions for noncompliance stems primarily from the funny money nature of private

mandated expenditures, which are purely accounting dollars and never show up in the agency's (or anyone's) bank balance. For this reason, there is no precise way of measuring costs and keeping an automatic control on the agency's running out of regulatory appropriations. Normal budget authority, by contrast, does exert automatic control because the bank balance of the agency keeps a running score on cumulative outlays. Putting the problem slightly differently, a regulatory agency could overrun its regulatory budget by $1 billion without anyone knowing it, for there is no automatic way of debiting a private cost against the agency that mandates it.

The funny money problem is not inherently fatal for the regulatory budget proposal. If costs were precisely measured, they could still be estimated and debits entered to agency accounts. Similarly, the ex ante accounting convention might prove an adequate substitute for a true bank statement. It is clear, however, that it will be difficult to provide an independent check on private sector compliance costs. In addition, because the chickens never come home to roost, the regulatory agency—with its superior expertise and greater resources—may be able to outwit or outwait outsiders and get away with it forever.

The methodological problems of estimating compliance costs are fundamental. Conceptually, the definition of regulatory cost is straightforward: it is the *marginal* cost to the economy of meeting a regulation. In some cases, such costs are easy to define: if a utility is forced to add a scrubber to an existing plant, the costs can be estimated with minimal difficulty. In a dynamic framework, however, the picture becomes more blurred. It may be difficult to anticipate changes in technology and, therefore, changes in costs over time. Assume, for example, that the costs of meeting environmental rules on a coal-fired electricity generating plant became so large that a utility decided to build a nuclear plant whose costs were virtually all mandated. What fraction of the nuclear power plant cost should be imputed to regulation? Or say that the next generation of coal-fired plants uses a more expensive but completely "clean" alternative process—such as fluidized bed combustion—that has no regulatory costs; does this imply the regulatory costs are nil?[11]

Another methodological issue concerns whether the budget should cover transfer payments in addition to resource costs and/or dead weight losses. Most of the discussion of the regulatory budget proposal has assumed that it would be limited only to resource cost effects. In many cases, however, the total distributional effects of a regulation significantly outweigh the direct (or even indirect) resource costs.[12] Restricting the budget to resource costs may therefore give a distorted picture of the actual impact of regulation. Indeed, it is for similar reasons that distributional effects are included in the federal expenditure budget.

Yet a third definitional issue is whether the costs measured in the budget would be limited only to "direct" costs or would also include "indirect" costs. Regulatory observers have generally assumed that the budget would measure only direct costs—the resources directly devoted to complying with regulations—because they are, in principle, the easiest to measure. There is no guarantee, however, that by controlling the

11. The analytical problems in measuring regulatory costs are very similar to those involved in calculating tax expenditures. See Stanley Surrey, *Pathways to Tax Reform* (Cambridge, Mass.: Harvard University Press, 1973). The latter involve an indirect calculation of revenue loss due to a feature of the tax code that permits incomes (or other tax bases) to be taxed at less than full rates. Since the "tax expenditure" is almost never actually the object of a transaction, complicated analytical questions arise. For example, the fact that interest on state and local bonds is not subject to taxation was recently estimated to represent $3.6 billion of tax expenditures for the year 1984. (Testimony of Joseph A. Pechman before the House Ways and Means Committee, February 18, 1982.) Yet, if taxes had actually been levied on this income, the relevant interest rates would have risen considerably, the income tax take would change as portfolios were reshuffled, and the ultimate effect on tax revenues would be different and probably lower.

It is interesting to note that these analytical problems do not faze those who use the tax expenditure concept; it is equally significant, however, that the concept has never had any practical significance in limiting tax loopholes.

12. This point was made to us by Robert R. Nordhaus with particular reference to the "incremental pricing" provisions of the 1978 Natural Gas Production Act. These provisions could redistribute billions of dollars from industry to consumers but have much lower resource costs.

direct costs from regulatory activity, society will be pursuing a desirable policy. If only direct costs are monitored, agencies will have incentives to shift costs to the "indirect category," however it may be defined, much as agencies now have the incentive to shift costs from the federal expenditure budget to private parties through regulatory action.

Given the foregoing methodological difficulties, it should be easy to understand why many of the estimates of the economic impact of regulatory programs presented in chapter 2 varied by such wide margins. In some cases, differences in estimates can be so wide as to render any effort to apply sanctions totally meaningless and potentially counterproductive. For example, Christopher deMuth and associates found extremely large discrepancies in cost estimates in the following instances:

> In 1978 the Consumer Product Safety Commission estimated the direct compliance cost of a proposed fabric flammability regulation for the furniture industry at $57 to $87 million a year. The American Textile Manufacturers Institute, in contrast, estimated direct compliance cost at $1.3 billion per year.
>
> In 1978 the Environmental Protection Agency estimated the annual direct compliance costs of a proposed ambient air quality standard for ozone at $6.9 to $9.5 billion per year. The RARG estimated those direct compliance costs at $14.3 to $18.8 billion per year.
>
> In February 1979, the Environmental Protection Agency estimated the costs of a proposed 1981 diesel engine particulate standard at a negative $160 per ton of particulates removed. The Council on Wage and Price Stability estimated this cost at a positive $4,740. For a proposed 1983 standard, the estimates per ton were $3,200 and $7,650, respectively.[13]

Discrepancies of this kind would almost certainly become the norm in disputes about regulatory costs under a regulatory budget procedure. The question thus arises as to whether sound

13. DeMuth et al., "The Regulatory Budget," pp. 46–47.

congressional decision-making can thrive in conditions of such uncertainty. There is no doubt, for example, that the budget process can use uncertainties to paper over some part of fundamental disagreements. Whatever theoretical advantages a budget process may have, therefore, in forcing tradeoffs, the pressure actually to make those tradeoffs could be attenuated by controversy surrounding the cost estimates, particularly in the early years of the process.

Because of this inherent uncertainty, some mechanism would have to be established to resolve such disputes. Widely respected bureaus like the General Accounting Office or the Congressional Budget Office could be charged with the task. However, the cost estimates could not accurately be made without extensive efforts by the government to audit private sector expenditures. Moreover, the auditing effort would have to be continuous; otherwise, no one would ever know if, at some point in the future, private expenditures ran over ceiling. Added to all these difficulties, some decisions would have to be made regarding judicial review of the cost determinations. To what extent should private parties have the right to challenge modifications made in rules required because mandated costs were found to exceed ceiling?

There are proposals that could help alleviate some of these problems. For example, Lawrence White has suggested the use of noncompliance penalties to help approximate private sector expenditures. Because firms would have an economic incentive to take steps to comply with a regulatory standard up to the point where the marginal cost of compliance equaled the cost of noncompliance (that is, the penalty times the probability that such a penalty would actually be imposed), the noncompliance penalty itself could help reveal how much was actually being spent by private firms to meet regulatory standards.[14]

While this scheme has its advantages, it cannot provide the *precise* estimates of private costs that would be called for under a formal budget procedure. First, as already suggested, it is not

14. Lawrence J. White, "Determining the Costs of Regulation: A Solution for the Regulatory Budget," *Regulation,* March/April 1980.

a certainty that noncompliance penalties would be imposed if a firm or individual did not comply with a regulation. Because it is difficult to determine the various probabilities of penalties for different regulations, it is correspondingly difficult to know the expected marginal cost of noncompliance facing different firms and individuals. Second, even if these probabilities were known, legal noncompliance would indicate only the likely costs of compliance *at the margin.* In the absence of some arbitrary assumptions about the cost schedules for compliance, there would be no way of knowing what *total level* of expenditures firms and individuals were making in an effort to comply with particular rules. Finally, such a procedure could not be used for brand-new regulatory programs (or, today, for virtually all programs) that had no noncompliance penalties in place.

An alternative idea for eliciting cost information would be to pay to firms and individuals regulatory tax credits (RTCs) for all mandated regulatory expenditures. The RTCs could be paid by the regulatory agency incurring them. Such a scheme would be doubly attractive: first, it would give some account of the total mandated regulatory costs; and second, it would allow Congress to give a handle to the budget by limiting the amount that agencies could pay out in regulatory tax credits. In the end, however, there would still remain the problem of measuring costs and assuring that cheating on the RTC did not occur. The result would be to shift the burden for accounting to the IRS, which, for the reasons already given, would have a far more difficult time auditing compliance costs than it now has uncovering income tax fraud and evasion.

If one approach has to be chosen, the most fruitful one is the ex ante approach discussed above. Such a route would resolve many of the thorniest problems but at the cost of allowing considerable accounting discretion and potential inaccuracy. It is questionable, therefore, that any gimmicks can be found to solve the funny money problem in a satisfactory way.

But even if regulatory costs could be measured easily, the designers of the regulatory budget would then face the difficult problem of deciding how to impose sanctions when mandated costs ran over ceiling. (These difficulties apply with much less force to the ex ante methodology.) How, for example, would the budgeteers determine which regulation caused the budget to exceed the authorized total? Where the budget is prepared in great detail, listing the authorized expenditure totals for individual regulations, it would be a simple matter to finger the offending regulation. Where the authorizations are more aggregated, however, the task could be more difficult. The problem would be especially acute where a single method of compliance was used to meet more than one regulatory standard. One pollution control device, for example, could be used to meet a wide range of emission standards. If the total expenditure for such devices helped to produce a cost overrun, which regulation should be modified to cure the problem?

A second sanctions-related problem arises in deciding exactly what steps should be taken when a budget ceiling is exceeded. Clearly, one possibility would be to revise the offending standard, beginning with a new notice of proposed rulemaking. Even though such a step might be feasible, the knowledge that all rules could be revised not only at the time of their scheduled sunset reviews but at any time after private sector costs were audited could introduce tremendous uncertainty into the investment process and thereby help to retard innovation and growth. This problem would be ameliorated by stating the budget ceilings in terms of life-time (rather than annual) costs, as we have already suggested, but would not be completely solved.

Another possible sanction that is sometimes mentioned in discussions of the regulatory budget would be the deduction of any cost overrun caused by existing regulations from *future* regulations. Thus, if the EPA's air quality program ran over ceiling by $5 billion for a given year, that excess could be used to penalize the budget total for the EPA's new regulatory proposals. The obvious problem with this procedure, however, is that there is no real way of policing future expenditures in a way that could make the cost overrun penalty effective. How would anyone truly know whether the EPA's future regulations paid that penalty? The agency could simply plan to overregulate and then, when forced to cut back by $5 billion, end up with the list of proposals it intended to issue in any case.

Yet a third sanction procedure would be to allow an agency

to offset its overruns against regulations whose costs were running below authorized ceiling. This would not really be a sanction but, in fact, more an accounting device that would leave some room in the process for budget overruns without imposing draconian penalties.

Finally, some type of sanction may have to be designed for those situations in which agencies expressly choose to spend *less* than the authorized expenditure ceiling—the regulatory impoundment problem. In the current climate, for example, if a regulatory budget process were in place, it would not be inconceivable for Congress to authorize, say, the EPA to mandate a higher total of private compliance costs than the current EPA would be willing to spend. The EPA could demonstrate this reluctance by setting performance standards at a far lower degree of stringency than Congress desired. Although Congress might not be able to force the EPA to tighten its standards immediately, the fact that compliance costs could reach a total considerably less than the authorized ceiling could alert Congress to the need for overriding any agency decision by setting the rule or standard itself.[15]

The ex ante methodology outlined above holds promise for resolving three of the four issues relating to sanctions (determining the violator, remedial steps, offsets, and impoundment) in a reasonable way. This is because under the ex ante approach the determination of costs is made *before* the regulation is issued. Therefore, even if a regulation turns out later to exceed the budget, it formally complies with the budget if its *projected* costs are consistent with the budget. Whether this approach is viable depends on the political tolerance for error and the willingness of elected officials to impose severe political sanctions against agencies or officials that consistently over- or underestimate costs.

These difficulties in designing sanctions highlight the im-

15. This has already happened in certain cases. For example, the fuel economy standards for passenger cars were written directly by Congress rather than by the EPA or NHTSA. The issue of impoundment, or nonenforcement, raises deeper problems when such action is generally perceived as unlawful.

portance of incorporating flexibility into the budget procedure. For example, we suggested above that it might be useful for Congress to delegate much of the authority to design and impose sanctions to the Executive, which would then be charged with reporting to Congress on a periodic basis the steps it had taken. This would permit the Executive to impose informal types of sanctions against offending agencies and administrators that often have better chances of success than rigid formulas written into statutes. In addition, flexibility can be introduced into the budget process if budget authorizations are stated in relatively broad categories. This would allow agencies greater freedom in taking remedial steps—by trading off the economic effects of various rules against each other—than a tightly drawn budget in which each regulatory proposal was given its own budget ceiling. Of course, such flexibility has its costs in terms of a weakening of congressional control. Nevertheless, given the wide range of uncertainty surrounding compliance costs produced by any particular regulation, the only feasible method of ever implementing a regulatory budget procedure will almost have to permit a substantial degree of flexibility and experimentation by all agencies subject to the budget process.

What should we conclude from this discussion of the main design issues? In our view, none of the problems—with regard to the scope of the regulatory budget, the nature of the dollar constraints, the manner of executive and congressional involvement in the process, and sanctions—is individually great enough to dissuade us of the desirability of a regulatory budget. But taken together, they are sufficiently severe to make it unwise to move toward a budget plan in one leap.

Nevertheless, because the budget is such a useful analogy for highlighting the defects in the current regulatory process, the key issue of regulatory policy design is to develop a method of oversight for the regulatory process that incorporates budget concepts in a workable fashion. It was arguably in this spirit that late in the Carter administration the OMB launched an effort to draft a Regulatory Cost Accounting Act. This would have required regulatory agencies at least to begin making, on a routine basis, the cost estimates that would enable a regulatory budget to be compiled, if not enforced. Others have suggested that the budget procedure be applied on an experimental basis to the regulations of one agency, with a view toward expanding over time the number of agencies covered by the procedure. Although this alternate approach has its attractions, it might be difficult to agree on the right guinea pig.

Either of the foregoing suggestions could serve an important function by helping to pave the way for the implementation of a full budget procedure. Both would stimulate public and professional interest not only in the cost estimates themselves but in the estimation techniques. It is conceivable that, over time, a consensus could be developed on the manner in which the funny money problem could be solved.

But can anything else be done in the meantime? If, as with the federal expenditure budget, sixty years are necessary to implement an acceptable regulatory budget procedure—and nothing else is done in the interim—a lot of regulations will continue to be issued in the absence of a workable control mechanism. The following chapter outlines a practical procedure that could fill this void.

7

The Legislated Regulatory Calendar

In the last two chapters, we have discussed current approaches to regulatory reform. We now present what we believe is a practical alternative to the regulatory budget. Specifically, we propose the implementation of a "legislated regulatory calendar" (LRC) which would require executive submission and legislative assent for major regulatory proposals but would not use dollar budgets as a way of constraining regulators' actions. While such a process does not have the elegance of a regulatory budget, it has the advantage of practicality and the prospect of restoring political accountability to the regulatory effort while enhancing incentives to pursue society's regulatory objectives more efficiently.

Congressional Approval of Regulatory Proposals

As we have argued throughout this book, the essential features of an effective control mechanism for regulatory decision-making are (1) that a systematic process of political review involving both the Executive and the Congress be established for regulatory decisions and (2) that the resulting process provide incentives for decision-makers to allocate resources toward the pursuit of regulatory objectives in an efficient manner. In theory, a regulatory budget would meet these objectives. In practice, however, the funny money aspect of the regulatory budget currently precludes dollar cost estimates from being used as an instrument of control. Without dollar constraints, the budget mechanism clearly lacks the incentives to decision-makers to regulate efficiently.

We believe that a practical oversight process for regulation can nevertheless be designed that promises at least some success in achieving the twin objectives of efficiency and political accountability. We label such a practical halfway house between the current chaos and a fully developed regulatory budget the *legislated regulatory calendar*. It would contain the following elements:

1. Each year the Executive would collate and submit to Congress a list of ''major'' Notices of Proposed Rulemakings (Notices), together with preliminary regulatory analyses of projected costs and benefits. As with a regulatory budget, a central executive office—presumably the OMB—would be charged with compiling the list after sifting through the submissions of proposals by the agencies.

2. Congress would consider the proposed list of regulatory proposals in much the same way that it would the regulatory budget discussed in the last chapter. A new standing committee in each chamber, the Regulatory Authorization Committee, would hold hearings on the views of the administration and interested parties on the proposed list. The authorization committees would then consider the list, modify it as necessary, and send the revised product to the floor of each chamber. A final list of authorized Notices would be approved by the full Congress; that is, the list would be passed by both chambers and signed by the President. No major rulemaking could proceed without such congressional authorization.

3. After congressional authorization, agencies would proceed with rulemaking, allowing for public comment. Depending on circumstances, agencies might be authorized to modify their proposals in response to comments made during the course of their rulemakings. The extent of the agencies' powers to change the proposals approved by Congress would be circumscribed either by a set of general guidelines or by a specific alternative proposal authorized by Congress. If an agency found that the rule it desired to issue went beyond or was not covered by the instructions given by Congress, it could include that proposal in the calendar submitted to Congress the following year.

These elements represent, of course, the bare outline of the process of legislative approval of regulatory proposals that we are recommending. Many of the important details that need to be filled in are set forth below.

1. Scope of the LRC Process

Many of the issues regarding the scope of the process have been discussed in connection with the regulatory budget, and the considerations for the calendar proposal are virtually identical.[1] For example, it is our view that only those proposals that are quasi-legislative in character should be subject to the process.[2] Similarly, as with the regulatory budget, the definition of a major regulation would have to contain a dollar threshold in order to prevent Congress from having to consider relatively minor regulatory proposals. It might be advantageous to set the dollar threshold initially at a relatively high level—say, $250 or $500 million—and then to adjust it downward as both the Congress and the Executive acquired experience with the process. Even at a threshold of $100 million, it would be highly unlikely, given prior experience, that the number of Notices on the annual list would exceed 100; more realistically the total would be in the neighborhood of fifty.[3]

1. The relevant discussion of scope is contained in chapter 6.

2. As we suggested in chapter 6, this would preferably be accomplished by defining precisely in the underlying legislation creating the LRC process those regulatory measures that would be subject to the process. To minimize the potential for litigation over the classification of individual rules, a subject we also examine below, the legislation creating the LRC process could simply rule out judicial review of decisions—by the Congress or the agencies—pertaining to the classification of which rules should be included in the calendar. Judicial review of such decisions would not be constitutionally necessary, since the Constitution protects the rights of interested parties to be notified of regulatory action and to be heard before the agency, and not the extent to which Congress has considered and analyzed the costs and benefits of a proposed rule. Of course, even without judicial review of such congressional decisions, parties would continue under the calendar process to be able to lodge court challenges under the Administrative Procedure Act to final rules promulgated by regulatory agencies.

3. Thus, the Reagan review program in 1981 turned up only forty-three major rules (see chapter 5).

Given the number and impact of regulations already on the books, an especially important aspect of the LRC process is the manner in which existing regulations would be considered. Under one proposal, existing regulations would not be subject to annual authorization but instead would automatically be reviewed when each agency came up for reauthorization. For agencies with long or permanent authorizations, however, this procedure would be ineffective. Consequently, an alternative method for considering existing regulations would be to incorporate in the LRC process a "sunset" procedure (proposed as part of the omnibus regulatory reform legislation discussed in chapter 5), which would require each agency to establish its own calendar for reviewing existing regulations. These calendars, which could also be made subject to congressional ratification, would permit the Congress to consider on an orderly basis the proposed revisions to existing rules that emerged from the agencies' sunset reviews.

Yet another issue of scope is the extent to which the legislation creating the LRC process would override or eliminate the timetables in many regulatory statutes that require agencies to issue certain rules by specific dates. In general, it seems preferable for the timetable for regulations to be set each year as part of the calendar process, thereby allowing a regular weighing of priorities and capabilities.[4] This may not be politically feasible, however, since certain constituencies may be successful in persuading Congress to retain the existing timetables that now may work in their favor. Clearly the retention of any such statutory deadlines detracts from the potential political and economic benefits to be gained from the LRC process.

4. This would also eliminate potential conflicts between the agenda-setting desires of the Executive or Congress and court-ordered deadlines for issuing certain rules. If the statutory deadlines were eliminated, courts would have few opportunities for setting and then enforcing such time schedules. Nevertheless, it should be understood that elimination of statutory deadlines would not deprive interested parties of the right to go to court to force a foot-dragging agency at least to place a particular rulemaking proposal on the LRC. Whether that particular rulemaking would proceed, however, would be a political decision to be rendered by Congress.

Finally, it is an open question whether the LRC list would contain only proposals by executive branch agencies or would also include proposals by independent agencies. Because OMB would have the power to strike or modify agency proposals in compiling the list, granting OMB jurisdiction over all regulatory proposals would remove some of the autonomy of the independent agencies. If continued autonomy is thought necessary, perhaps the best approach would be the direct submission of proposals to Congress by the independent agencies themselves.

2. Form of Legislative Assent

The second, and perhaps most difficult, set of design issues relates to the manner in which Congress would consider, and assent to, the list of proposals submitted through the LRC. In particular, which committees should participate in the regulatory authorization process? How much freedom should Congress have to modify or supplement the proposed list, either in committees or on the floor?

In chapter 6, we discussed in connection with the regulatory budget the contrasting features of centralized committees, such as the regulatory authorization committees that would be part of the LRC, versus the individual oversight committees.[5] Specifically, we suggested that while concentrating both budgetary and appropriations authority in central budget committees would be advantageous from an administrative point of view, such an outcome might be politically unrealistic. The same would be true of a regulatory authorization procedure, since each of the existing oversight committees could be expected to protect its current authority over the individual regulatory agencies within its jurisdiction. At the same time, however, it would be a signal advantage if the entire review process were transferred to central authorizing committees whose members could develop broader interests and greater expertise in regulatory matters generally and with respect to the LRC process in particular.

We see two possible solutions to this conflict. Under one alternative, the proposed list of Notices included in the calendar

5. See p. 149.

could, at least initially, be referred solely to the new regulatory authorization committees, provided the list itself were relatively short. This could occur, for example, if the process were started with a relatively high dollar threshold defining what constitutes a major regulatory proposal. As that threshold was lowered and the number of Notices on the proposed list thereby increased, the administrative—as well as political—case for referring a portion, if not all, of the Notices to the appropriate oversight committees would become stronger.

This first alternative may be judged by individual congressmen still to cede too much power to the regulatory authorization committees. For this reason, a second possibility would be *joint* referrals, under which the entire list of Notices would at the outset be referred to the regulatory authorization committees while individual Notices also were distributed among the specific oversight committees with relevant jurisdiction. For example, a proposed worker safety standard on the executive list would be referred both to the authorization committees and to the OSHA oversight committees in each chamber. The authorization and oversight committees would, of course, attempt to work out their differences before sending recommendations to the full floor. Where agreement could not be reached—when, for example, the two committees disagreed as to whether a particular Notice should be authorized—both recommendations would be forwarded to the floor, where the full House or Senate would be required to resolve the difference.

However many committees actually became involved in the authorization process, the most important aspect of legislative involvement is how the Notices on the proposed regulatory calendar would actually be considered. The major difficulty with congressional involvement in the regulatory process stems from the inertial tendency of legislatures. It is a fact of political life that, because *changes* in legislative policy must overcome a large number of hurdles, a presumption is generally accorded to the status quo. This inertial aspect of the legislative process has both positive and negative implications for our LRC proposal. On the one hand, under the LRC process a costly regulation with a small constituency would have greater difficulty surviving congressional and agency scrutiny than under the current process. On the other hand, the LRC procedure could permit powerful lobbies to stymie worthwhile regulations with dispersed beneficiaries.

This inertia in congressional deliberations clearly could be overcome by placing restrictions on the amendment process, which could otherwise allow narrow constituencies to have a disproportionate effect on the outcome of congressional deliberations on the list of proposals set forth in the calendar. For example, under one type of restriction, congressional committees, as well as the full Congress, could consider each proposed regulation on a take-it-or-leave-it basis. Although this procedure might seem unnecessarily restrictive, regulatory agencies are clearly in a better position than the Congress to develop specific regulatory proposals and their accompanying regulatory analyses. Indeed, Congress has established regulatory agencies precisely in order to fulfill such functions. In contrast, as we discuss further below, Congress is better suited for making broader policy decisions, which would be posed in concrete terms by the regulatory proposals included in the calendar.

An alternative restriction would be to limit floor amendments to the proposals recommended by the regulatory authorization committees and/or specific oversight committees. This approach would differ from the one just described in that it would permit the committees to recommend changes to individual rules but would foreclose the addition of further amendments on the floor of each chamber. The clear advantage of this second approach is that, because the proposed calendar would contain a wide range of proposals, there would be strong incentives for Congress not to let it languish in indefinite idleness. The principal disadvantage is that, because a zealous committee could very well include a number of regulations on the list that it, but not the Executive, wanted to issue in the coming year, the limited amendment process could prevent the full Congress from correcting errors believed to have been made in committee.

New sets of legislative strategies would clearly emerge if

the list of proposed regulations were considered on a limited amendment or perhaps even a no-amendment and expedited basis. Such restrictions on congressional deliberations would very likely cause the content of regulatory proposals to be designed in negotiations between the regulatory agency and senior members and staffs of the regulatory authorization committees. Exactly such an outcome has already occurred in the trade area; the 1979 Multinational Trade Negotiations were conducted by the Executive with substantial input and guidance from key Senate and House committees. It is widely recognized that the process of legislative consideration of the trade negotiations worked extremely well. Indeed the 1979 trade act, which ratified the negotiated results, used an expedited procedure and passed Congress almost unanimously.

If, notwithstanding this successful precedent, the limited amendment approach is judged to provide too little leeway for congressional maneuvering, there are ways in which congressional deliberations on the proposed calendar could be made more flexible. In particular, Congress could require that each proposed notice contain either alternative proposals or a range of possible regulations. The accompanying regulatory analyses would be required to contain projections of costs and benefits of the alternatives. Such ranges would permit Congress either to choose among alternatives or to express a preference as to whether the final rule should be at the more or less stringent end of the spectrum.

By requiring the Executive to submit alternatives for each of the Notices included on the list together with pertinent cost and benefit information, some of the features of a regulatory budget might emerge; that is, Congress would make barterlike choices among regulations rather than reallocate dollars. It is more likely, however, that the practical drawbacks to the presentation of alternatives would seriously limit their effectiveness. A clear danger of the alternatives approach, for example, is that the Executive could manipulate the congressional deliberation on its proposals by cleverly presenting the various alternatives in such a way that its preferred proposals looked good only because the alternatives looked so bad. Congress would then be confronted with the familiar three decision boxes in which the two extreme and badly designed proposals carefully straddle the clearly preferred central option. Another problem would arise when the regulatory issues were multidimensional, since then the decision alternatives themselves would not be neatly arrayed along a single spectrum.

These shortcomings are not just theoretical. Earlier experiments with the use of alternatives—by the Bureau of the Budget in the late 1960s and under the current expenditure budget process—show that gaming impedes the effectiveness of the exercise. One variation familiar to congressional observers is the "Washington Monument game"—placing such undesirable alternatives as closing down the Washington Monument in the same package with other, less controversial proposals to ensure that the whole package is voted down.

In the end, we believe that the problems with the presentation and deliberation of alternative proposals are sufficiently serious to tip the scales in favor of an expedited, limited (or no-amendment) approach as the appropriate method for involving Congress in regulatory decision-making. We believe that such a mechanism would ensure that both the executive and legislative branches would be involved in the regulatory process in a meaningful way without at the same time disrupting the development of needed rules. We recognize, of course, that fewer complications would exist if only the executive branch were involved in the process. On the other hand, consideration of regulatory proposals without congressional participation would be inconsistent with a primary objective of the LRC proposal: *to restore political accountability to the regulatory process.* In addition, a calendar process as complete as the one we have described, which was run solely in the executive branch, would very likely represent an unacceptable delegation of legislative authority to the Executive. We prefer a legislative assent mechanism as part of any major regulatory reform effort and believe that a workable legislative procedure, such as that described above, can be devised and implemented.

3. Review after Rules Have Been Promulgated

The third set of design issues centers on the possibility of providing for congressional review of rules after they are adopted by the agencies. Under the process we have described, Congress would have no role after the agencies made their final decisions (except that Congress could, of course, pass a law overriding a final rule). We believe that such a role for Congress is appropriate. The legislative assent mechanism we have described is closely analogous to the current expenditure budget process in which Congress authorizes, say, the construction of an MX missile, while the Department of Defense is charged with choosing the vendor. By authorizing a particular rulemaking to proceed, Congress would perform much the same function in the regulatory arena.[6]

A potentially more controversial subject is the role of judicial review of final agency rules developed under the LRC process. Ideally, congressional involvement in the regulatory process should be designed in a manner that does not disturb the rights of interested parties to due process under the Constitution, while at the same time it enhances the political accountability for and efficiency of final regulatory decisions. We believe that the proposed LRC process meets these twin objectives. At the same time, care must be taken at the various points in the process to ensure that the opportunity for judicial review does not degenerate, as it has under the National Environmen-

---

6. Congressional control over the outcomes of rulemakings would be enhanced, of course, by permitting Congress to veto final rules before they become effective. We do not favor the legislative veto, however, for the reasons already given in chapter 5.

An alternative to the veto would be to permit Congress to require agencies to obtain reauthorization of rulemakings where the final rules deviate "significantly" from either the original proposals (as seen by the GAO or OMB) or from the alternative preferred by Congress. The problem with this procedure, however, is that it could stretch out the rulemaking process interminably —perhaps, in some cases, degenerating into a game of cat and mouse between the agency and Congress. Indeed, it would give an antiregulatory branch the chance to hold up rules on the pretext that the final rule deviated significantly from the authorized proposals, when in fact any such change between the proposal and the final rule was minor.

tal Policy Act, into simply a tool for obstruction and delay. Thus, if it is decided that agencies should be allowed to modify the proposals authorized by Congress, the guidelines written by Congress should be sufficiently clear so that the issue of whether a particular change is permitted by Congress is not a source of endless litigation. One particular approach, for example, might be to require Congress to reauthorize *any* change made by the agency. A less rigid approach would provide a sufficiently broad range of outcomes in the original authorization so as to allow for flexibility in the development of the final rules. We expect that if the LRC process were implemented, agencies would, in fact, choose this latter course by stating their proposals in terms that would allow them flexibility to shape any final rule to specific comments subsequently submitted by interested parties. Of course, where no changes in a proposal are recommended, or where the proposal is itself rejected, the LRC process provides no greater opportunity for judicial review than exists under the current process.

However Congress chooses to structure its involvement, the additional participation in regulatory decision-making by Congress provided through the LRC should streamline and simplify the tasks of those courts that are called upon to decide challenges to agency rules. Substantive challenges to agency rules typically require courts to decide whether an agency lacks either the statutory authority or supporting evidence for promulgating a particular rule. While the LRC would not affect the agencies' evidentiary burdens, which are discharged by receiving public comments after proposals are announced, the calendar process would be likely to have a significant effect on would-be challengers who allege that a rule violates the agency's statutory authorization.

Specifically, congressional consideration of agency proposals provides, in effect, ongoing legislative interpretation of the underlying regulatory statutes that authorize such rulemakings in the first instance. These interpretations, in the form of specific congressional votes and any recommended changes to specific proposals, would place a congressional imprimatur of lawfulness on the rules authorized through the LRC, which should make reviewing courts more hesitant to overturn them and thereby deter judicial challenges in the first instance. Continuing congressional involvement would provide the agencies clearer and more regular guidance about Congress's legislative intentions.[7] This improved clarity should, in turn, reduce the number of challenges to final agency actions and thereby remove an important source of the delay that now plagues the development of many rules.

4. Emergency Rules

A final design issue concerns emergency rulemakings. The foregoing legislative procedure would easily work in the case of routine regulatory proposals, which ordinarily require a substantial degree of lead time for fact investigation. In certain instances, however, an agency needs to promulgate an emergency rule to address a particularly pressing problem. We propose that, under limited circumstances, agencies be permitted to promulgate such emergency regulations without first obtaining congressional authorization provided that, in the subsequent year, the Executive submit to Congress as part of its list a Notice proposing a permanent rule to replace the emergency provisions.[8]

To sum up, our proposed process of a legislated regulatory calendar would contain the following specific elements in addition to the general design features already outlined:

1. The process would be limited to major, quasi-legislative regulatory proposals. The definition of a "major" rule could be adjusted to control the number of regulatory proposals considered.

2. Although it would be preferable to refer the list of Notices proposed by the Executive solely to the regulatory authorization com-

7. Again, it bears emphasis that the agencies must still back any final rule they issue with sufficient evidentiary support.

8. If it is decided that the independent agencies would be responsible for submitting their proposals directly and not through the OMB, the independents would also be required to submit the "permanent" versions of their emergency rules.

mittees in each chamber, joint referral to individual oversight committees might have to be adopted.

3. Congress would consider the legislated regulatory calendar on an expedited, limited amendment basis. Regulatory authorization committees would forward, within, say, sixty legislative days, a list of proposed regulations to the floor. The regulatory proposals would then be voted on a limited or perhaps no-amendment basis within a prescribed period.

4. No major, quasi-legislative rulemaking could proceed without congressional authorization.

The complete process for approving regulatory proposals is illustrated in figure 7.1, which traces the development of a regulatory proposal, such as the EPA's sulfur scrubbing rule, through the various stages of the procedure.

Before leaving the description of our LRC proposal, we want to call attention to a variation of the legislative calendar process that would concentrate to a greater extent than ours on congressional consideration of broad priorities and to a lesser degree on the deliberation over specific regulatory proposals.[9] Such an alternative process is motivated by the view that congressional capabilities are more limited than we suggest here, as elaborated further below.

More specifically, in place of congressional consideration of the Notices of Proposed Rulemakings developed by regulatory agencies, this alternative would limit Congress to considering broad outlines of the agencies' regulatory priorities, together with available estimates of costs and benefits of regulatory activity in various areas. For example, the EPA could describe its intended efforts in the areas of air pollution, water pollution (distinguishing perhaps between toxic and conventional pollutants), and hazardous wastes; OSHA could describe its intentions regarding worker exposure to toxic substances; and the NHTSA could submit its plans for regulating cars and tires. To make all of these reports more concrete, the agencies

9. The outline of such a proposal has been offered to the authors by George Eads, who served as a member of the CEA from March 1979 through January 1981.

Figure 7.1. The Development of a Major Rule under the Current Process and under the Legislated Regulatory Calendar

CURRENT PROCESS:

LEGISLATED REGULATORY CALENDAR:

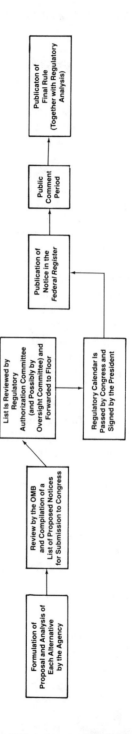

could submit agendas of planned rulemakings, together with preliminary cost and benefit information, in a manner roughly analogous to the summary information provided by the regulatory calendar published by the Regulatory Council during the Carter administration. Congress would examine the proposed agendas and the broad policy issues and then would pass a joint resolution and report affirming, questioning, or criticizing the priorities chosen by the various agencies.

As a control device, this alternative priority oversight procedure clearly would be far weaker than the LRC. Congress would have available to it considerably less information about the content and projected impact of the regulatory proposals offered by agencies and would thus be unable to exert a significant degree of control over the shape of the rules subsequently developed. In addition, the legal status of the process could be somewhat murky if Congress were only authorizing the issuance of a report and resolution rather than a legally binding statute (as in the case of the legislated regulatory calendar). And finally, there is no implicit budget framework, as there would be with the more elaborate calendar process described here, inducing agencies or branches to trim back wasteful programs. The principal advantage of the priority oversight procedure, however, is that it may be easier for Congress to adopt and implement than the LRC, since Congress would be required simply to express its views on broad policy directions rather than on specific proposals.

Addressing the Current Defects through a Process of Congressional Authorization

The constraints on regulatory decision-making provided under the LRC process suggested above clearly are not as tight as under a regulatory budget, since mandated expenditures cannot be used as the central instrument of control. As a result, the LRC process does not permit as precise supervision of the regulatory process as the proposed regulatory budget. Nevertheless, by requiring Congress to go beyond the enactment of vague regulatory legislation and to monitor directly the methods by which the blanks in such legislation are filled in through rulemaking, a process of congressional authorization of regulatory proposals goes a long way toward addressing the defects in the current process.

It is clear that involving both the Executive Office of the President and the Congress on a *systematic basis* in making fundamental regulatory decisions would substantially enhance political accountability for those decisions. What may not be as clear, however, is that this result would be achieved by responding to each of the major rationales often given for congressional delegation of regulatory authority in the first instance.

For example, as we have discussed at various points in earlier chapters, delegation has frequently been justified on the grounds that Congress does not and cannot hope to possess sufficient information about many of the details of particular regulatory problems at the time it enacts authorizing legislation establishing a regulatory program. Such fact-finding has instead been expressly delegated to administrative agencies. A problem with the current regulatory process, however, is that once such information has been gathered on a case-by-case basis, the agencies have been permitted to formulate policy in each of those cases without sufficient congressional supervision. The proposed process of legislative approval would alleviate that defect by reinserting Congress into the regulatory process at the point where sufficient information about a particular application of the underlying statute has been obtained to permit the formulation of a proposed course of action.

A second rationale for delegation is that administrative agencies are believed to have greater expertise in any given regulatory area than Congress. While this is likely to be true as to the fact gathering and evaluation functions involved in regulatory decisions, the existence of such expertise cannot justify the abstention of Congress from the important *policy* judgments that must be made in issuing regulations. In making these policy judgments, *elected officials* are better able—and, in a democracy, more suited—to make broad allocational decisions than are agency bureaucrats. Moreover, by concentrating responsibility for assembling the list of regulatory proposals in central offices within both the Executive and the Congress, the congressional authorization process would create a new set of regulatory experts who would not be tied to any specific regulatory mission.

This transfer of authority and responsibility away from the single interest regulatory agencies highlights a third advantage of authorizing regulatory proposals. Whatever normative rationales may be advanced to justify the delegation of regulatory authority to the administrative agencies, it can be argued that, in fact, Congress has chosen to delegate the filling in of statutory blanks in order to avoid the hard work or unpleasant political issues that are frequently raised in the process. There are strong reasons for believing that a regulatory authorization procedure structured in the manner we have suggested would continue to allow Congress to delegate the tiresome work while providing a budgetlike framework that would more easily permit Congress to make important allocational decisions.

It must be emphasized, but we will not belabor, that we are not espousing a naive view that the objectives of members of Congress are to pass the most cost-beneficial programs; nor that there is a kind of political invisible hand operating that assures that the outcome of congressional deliberations will accord with the wishes of the average voter.

Our view is that congressmen have an uncertain mixture of ideology, national interest, and self-survival in mind when they take positions. Viewed as collective decisions, the outcomes provide the best available way of guiding broad national priorities—at least as compared to unchecked executive or agency decision-making. The major constraint on using congressional decision-making is the very great scarcity of true deliberative time. For this reason, less important issues do not get resolved well in the congressional decision process: they are either ignored or turned over to the parochial interests of a particular committee or member. This view suggests that congressional involvement will work best on setting the overall regulatory agenda and poorly on narrow issues, such as those that would be triggered by legislative vetoes.

The LRC proposal is designed to take advantage of these

features of congressional decision-making by enabling Congress to decide regulatory priorities in the concrete setting of specific regulatory proposals and their accompanying analyses. Since the calendar each year would consist largely of social regulatory programs, the LRC would enable Congress to decide in a structured environment the priorities to be given to reducing the variety of risks that the nation's regulatory programs have been designed to reduce. As one federal judge has recently stated, such decisions are precisely of the kind that, under our form of government, Congress should make:

> If our republican form of democracy means anything, it means that the people, through their representatives, shall make the basic decisions controlling their lives. *The type and extent of the risks acceptable in their lives is perhaps the most basic of all those decisions.* The power to make those final decisions should not be even indirectly vested in a few unelected bureaucrats, who have virtual life tenure in their jobs, under review by a few unelected judges who have a constitutional life tenure (emphasis added).[10]

The contrast between the present process of regulatory decision-making and the process that would be established by the LRC can be illustrated by comparing the development under the two systems of a single regulation, say, a proposed worker safety standard. Under the current process, the regulation would be developed by OSHA after it received comments primarily from labor groups and business interests. The choice would be made by *nonelected* officials in an environment where those who would potentially benefit from the regulation would be opposed by those who would be required to bear its cost. The only interested parties not generally represented would be consumers, who ultimately bear the burden of regulatory action.

The process of legislative authorization we have outlined would significantly change the method by which the proposed worker standard would be considered and then promulgated.

10. See testimony of Judge Howard Markey, House Committee on Science and Technology, Risk/Benefit Analysis in the Legislative Process, H. Rep. No. 71, 96th Cong., 1st Sess. at 99 (1979).

Under the LRC, the Executive and Congress would have to weigh not only the potential benefits and costs of the worker safety standard itself but could also be expected to consider the potential benefits and costs of other proposed standards as well as other approaches to the problem. Both branches would have the means, and clearly the incentive, to consider the impact of regulations on efficiency, real incomes, and inflation. Moreover, both branches would then be able to assess specific regulatory proposals in the context of *other* regulatory programs—environmental, antidiscrimination, consumer protection, and so on—each of which requires expenditure of private sector resources. The nature of the regulatory decision under the LRC, therefore, is thus not whether any *particular group* should be entitled to a specific level of regulatory protection but rather which regulatory objectives should have *prior claim* to the limited quantity of private resources available. Congress could thus recommend relaxation of a particular worker safety proposal while, *at the same time,* recommending the strengthening of another environmental or antidiscrimination proposal. The combination or packaging of regulatory decisions, coupled with a change in the locus of the decision-making, would allow the Executive and Congress to shift programs and priorities, much as now occurs for expenditure decisions.

This packaging effect taken alone will clearly have a less powerful effect on regulatory decisions than a regulatory budget constraint. For example, what is to prevent Congress from simply ratifying the sum total of the individual regulatory actions taken by the myriad regulatory agencies, much as it does, implicitly, today? Given that the authorization process proposed here expressly rejects the use of dollar ceilings to constrain the total of private expenditures mandated by regulation, how would it provide the budgetary discipline required to force Congress and the Executive to make the necessary tradeoffs?

We believe that the proposed LRC process contains features at two levels that would produce constraints on regulatory decision-making. Overall discipline would grow naturally out of the transfer of power from the individual agencies and committees to the regulatory authorization committees in Congress and to the OMB in the Executive. Moreover, like the President's annual budget message, the release of the list of proposed regulatory notices would become a major political event. For the first time, the nation would have collected in one place its annual agenda for major regulatory action together with projections of benefits and costs. Just as the level of federal expenditures and the projections of federal deficit have become the focus of national attention, the total projected impact of the President's proposed regulatory program would also assume major importance. If that impact were deemed too high, public pressure would be brought to reduce it. Conversely, if the total commitment were deemed insufficient, it could be increased.

The related concern has been expressed to us that it would be difficult to find any rational basis for obtaining a consensus as to the proper range of overall mandated compliance costs. In the expenditure area, there are good macroeconomic reasons for changing expenditures or taxes in any period. What arguments can Congress appeal to for limiting the private sector expenditures mandated by federal regulation?

Such limits can be defended on two grounds. First, just as the federal government makes a *political* choice in deciding what fraction of society's resources to devote to public objectives through direct expenditures, the government should make a choice with regard to resources allocated through regulation. Many, for example, now feel that 23 percent of the GNP is either too much or too little to spend directly through the federal government. Similar feelings can develop about the percentage of GNP devoted to meeting regulatory objectives, once these cost estimates are routinely performed and made available. Once the notions of how much should be spent on regulations take root, there will be forces to economize, and the very weakest programs are likely to be weeded out.

Second, decisions about overall ceilings on mandated private expenditures will promote professional interest and research into the total effects of the regulatory effort on key macroeconomic variables, perhaps one day paralleling the interest of economists in the macroeconomic effects of expenditures, taxes, and deficit levels. Similar interest is likely to be expressed by private investors, many of whom follow and are concerned about the diversion of potential investment funds into government projects. The level of private expenditures required to meet federal standards—and the issue of what might be called "regulatory crowding out"—would be likely to attract the same level of attention. If it turns out that regulatory crowding out is significant, as we suspect, this would add force to those proponents of greater efficiency in regulatory programs.

In short, even though the regulatory authorization process would not rely explicitly on private mandated expenditure ceilings to control regulatory activity precisely, the total projected impact of the list of regulatory notices would itself be significant and thus would transform the nature of the political debate surrounding regulatory issues. Under the current process, there is simply no mechanism whereby the public or its elected representatives can become aware of the total impact—either in terms of costs or of benefits—of federal regulatory activity. One recent survey indicates that the public is currently ill-informed about federal regulatory activities: half of those interviewed could not name even one regulation that affected them or their families, and only 17 percent knew that the executive branch is primarily responsible for writing federal regulations (47 percent thought Congress was).[11] A process of regulatory authorization would elevate the public importance of regulatory issues and alter public perception of those issues by bringing to the surface the information and issues surrounding that total impact. The result, we believe, would be the gradual formation of a set of views about the appropriate level of regulatory activity, as measured by a range of projected private sector compliance costs and benefits. Although such views would not be as precise or as binding as the budget ceiling is for federal expenditures, they would, as a practical matter, be sufficiently concrete to require decision-makers in both branches to make

11. The survey was taken by the Gallup organization on behalf of the League of Women Voters and the Bendix Corporation. The results were reported in *Regulation,* July/August 1982, p. 7.

tradeoffs between regulatory objectives and programs and, ultimately, to trim the more wasteful projects.

The regulatory authorization process could also be expected to lead to constraints at a more disaggregated level. In the formal description of the process, we have suggested that the Executive—primarily the OMB—would be charged with preparing a suggested list of regulatory notices that would subsequently be considered by the Congress. In practice, however, the executive agencies, as well as the OMB, would seek to lay the political foundation for congressional acceptance of those notices by cooperating with the regulatory authorization committees in the process of actually *developing* the proposed list. In the interests of presenting less costly proposals, there would very likely be a tendency to economize on regulatory outlays, particularly on the inefficient programs.

It can be argued that such a result would too greatly politicize the regulatory process. But that is precisely the objective. The regulatory process *is* a political process. A procedure of legislated authorization provides a structure in which the *elected* decide important regulatory issues without becoming overwhelmed by complexities. Indeed, we suspect that such a procedure is the only practical method by which both the Executive and Congress can reassert their roles in directing the allocation of society's resources toward regulatory objectives.

To be sure, there is still much for Congress to do in revamping individual regulatory statutes to provide greater freedom to balance costs and benefits and to introduce economic incentives to replace restrictive standards. As we discussed in chapter 4, these statutory restrictions now impede the attainment of regulatory goals in an efficient manner and would thus frustrate the efficiency-enhancing aspects of the regulatory authorization procedure suggested here.

At the same time, the implementation of an authorization procedure would itself help to lay the foundation for change of those statutes by exposing each year to public view the inefficiencies of the various statutory restrictions. For example, when advocates of more stringent rules on toxic substances are told that a particular regulation cannot be tightened because an

OSHA standard set under a "no balancing" statutory mandate is already imposing a heavy private sector burden, a new constituency will have been created for requiring a balancing of costs against benefits in the OSH Act. Similarly, just as proponents of social programs become extremely interested in the design of the MX missile, so when elected representatives discover that billions can be shaved off the total compliance cost burden by authorizing greater use of economic incentives, such as emission taxes, noncompliance fees, and the like, a new constituency may conceivably spring up to support experimentation with economic incentives. Indeed, these constituencies for efficiency will be strengthened by the creation of the regulatory authorization committees, whose natural interests would favor steps that would promote the efficient attainment of society's many regulatory objectives.

Conclusion

Americans are frustrated with the inability of their political leaders to cope effectively with the problems that now plague the regulatory process. The airways and journals are filled with proposals that, at best, would provide only temporary and superficial solutions and, at worst, could so disrupt the process that the costs of action would far outweigh the benefits.

We have argued throughout that the proper remedy must treat the root causes of the current difficulties—the nearly wholesale delegation of authority over regulatory matters to a wide range of additional branches of government not directly accountable to the political process. We have suggested a process of congressional authorization of regulatory proposals as an interim solution. The regulatory authorization process would reassert congressional and presidential authority over regulatory decisions at the stages in the process where participation by each branch would be most effective. Furthermore, it would do so in a way that would encourage public decision-makers to weigh both the overall consequences of their regulatory actions and the relative merits of specific regulatory incentives. We believe that in such an environment of greater political involvement, over the long run, more effective and balanced regulation will emerge.

Sources and Brief Description for Tables 2.4, 2.5, 2.6, and 2.7

Table 2.4. Cost of Pollution Control Programs

(a) "Pollution Abatement and Control Expenditures." U.S. Department of Commerce, Bureau of Economic Analysis, *Survey of Current Business,* February 1982.

These are estimates of total pollution abatement and control expenditures. No attempt has been made to adjust these figures downward to account for expenditures that would have been made in the absence of regulation. The estimates include total annual investment.

(b) *The Cost of Clean Air and Clean Water, Report to the Congress August 1979.* U.S. Environmental Protection Agency, EPA 230/3-79-001, pp. vii–xii.

These are estimates of the annualized incremental costs incurred on account of the Clean Air and Clean Water Acts. They are "the result of engineering estimates . . . based on the assumed application of existing technology, and are developed by various techniques such as the use of 'model' plants or actual data on existing plants. Various other assumptions are used, such as the utilization of an 'average' air pollution regulation typical of all state implementation plans. The assumptions are judged to result in an overstatement of costs, since no allowances are made for in process changes or technological innovation, either of which might reduce the costs of pollution control."

(c) *Environmental Quality: The Ninth Annual Report of the Council on Environmental Quality.* Washington, D.C., 1978, pp. 424–30, 448.

"This year's cost estimates were provided primarily by the EPA and are consistent with its analysis of the costs of clean air and clean water" (note 24, p. 448.) Thus, all that has been presented is CEQ's estimate of solid waste costs, which is on a comparable theoretical basis to (b).

(d) *Pollution Abatement and Control Expenditures, 1977,* U.S. Department of Commerce, Bureau of the Census, MA-200(77)-1.

These estimates are for the manufacturing sector only and are on a comparable theoretical basis to (a).

(e) Denison, Edward, "Pollution Abatement Programs: Estimates of Their Effect Upon Output per Unit Input," *Survey of Current Business,* January 1978.

These estimates are based on BEA data and refer to annualized incremental costs for private nonresidential business only. The total is less than the sum of the parts due to the value of energy and materials reclaimed. "Solid Waste and Other" includes payments to use public sewer systems.

(f) Weidenbaum, M. and DeFina, R., *The Cost of Federal Regulation of Economic Activity.* Washington, D.C.: American Enterprise Institute, 1978.

Weidenbaum and DeFina's estimate for 1976, $8.176 billion, was inflated to 1977 dollars using the implicit price deflator for gross domestic product. Their estimate in turn is based on an inflated value of earlier CEQ figures and refers to incremental, gross annual costs.

(g) Crandall, R., "Federal Government Initiatives to Reduce the Price Level," *Brookings Papers on Economic Activity,* no. 2. Washington, D.C.: Brookings Institution, 1978.

This estimate refers to the prospective annual incremental cost, assuming full enforcement of regulations and excludes mobile source pollutant controls and the cost of public water treatment and solid waste management.

(h) Arthur Anderson and Company, *The Cost of Government Regulation Study for the Business Roundtable.* New York: Arthur Anderson and Company, March 1979.

This estimate is of incremental expenditure based upon the determinations of forty-eight surveyed companies of costs in excess of what "actions they would have taken in the absence of regulation." Capital costs are accounted for on an accrual basis.

(i) The total takes the highest and lowest figure of those that attempt to estimate costs for all programs. The highest figure—from source (a)—is total rather than incremental. The lowest—from source (e)—attempts to make these incremental costs and annualizes the investment outlays.

Table 2.5. Costs of Health and Safety Regulation

(a) Denison, E., *Accounting for Slower Economic Growth: The United States in the 1970s.* Washington, D.C.: Brookings Institution, 1979.

These are estimates of incremental capital and opportunity costs. The estimate for automobile expenditures is based upon BLS series. The estimate for mining safety is based upon an attribution of the productivity drop in mining to increased safety regulation and so ought to be seen as an upper bound.

(b) Peltzman, S., "An Evaluation of Consumer Protection Legislation: the 1962 Drug Amendments." *Journal of Political Economy* (October 1973): 1049–91.

This estimate is of reduced consumer surplus due to decreased innovation and price rivalry. The author attributes the entire decline in the introduction of new drugs after 1962 to the 1962 FDA amendments. He further values the cost of fewer new drugs as the decrease in demand for new drugs, drawn from data supplied by pharmacies on their sales and prices. The study assumes the value of a new drug to be the value that would have been paid for it and thus ignores any questions regarding the efficacy of drugs.

(c) National Highway Traffic Safety Administration, "The Contribution of Automobile Regulation," June 1978.

(d) Denison, "Pollution Abatement Programs."

This study attributes the entire decline in productivity growth since 1969 to the cost of implementing the Mine Safety Act.

(e) *Nuclear Power Regulation*, U.S. Department of Energy, Policy Study, vol. 10, DOE/EIA-0201/10.

The cost estimate is derived by assuming that recent increases in the real costs of constructing nuclear plants were due entirely to the effects of regulation. Thus, total nuclear power capacity in 1990 is estimated to be between 90 and 128 gigawatts electric (GWE). The cost of building a nuclear plant rose from $560 million per GWE for plants operating in 1979 to $1185 million per GWE for new reactors (estimated in 1981, both in 1977 prices). Assuming the increase is due to regulation and that all new and old units will be built or upgraded to current standards provides estimates of total costs of $41 to $58 billion. Dividing these amounts evenly over a fifteen-year period from 1975 to 1990 yields the estimates in table 2.5.

(f) The totals in the range take the high and low from each source above.

Table 2.6. Costs of Economic Regulation

(a) Weidenbaum, M. and DeFina, R., *The Cost of Federal Regulation of Economic Activity.* Washington, D.C.: American Enterprise Institute, 1978.

As mentioned in the text, this study uses a similar methodology to the one employed here. As such, it was used as a reference to many of the studies cited here, particularly for economic regulation.

(b) Moore, T. G., "Deregulating Surface Freight Transportation," in Phillips, A., ed., *Promoting Competition in Regulated Markets.* Washington, D.C.: Brookings Institution, 1975, pp. 55–98.

Citing Peck, Harbeson, and Friedlaender, this estimate is of increased costs to consumers for given levels of service plus losses incurred due to inefficient choice of transportation mode and pricing above marginal costs. It does not include secondary distortions or losses from reduced innovation.

(c) Friedlaender, Ann, "The Social Costs of Regulating the Railroads," *American Economic Review* 41 (May 1971): 234.

This estimate is of the sum of the costs of inefficient pricing (estimated in earlier study by author) and the cost of excess capacity. The author uses George Borts's theory that the difference between the long and short run elasticity determines the excess capacity. She estimates these elasticities from the cost figures from eighty-eight railroads over time. Excess capacity translates into social cost either through increased operating costs or decreased value of output. Friedlaender's 1969 figures were updated to 1977 by multiplying the welfare loss by the ratio of 1977 to 1969 operating revenues.

(d) Jantscher, Gerald R., *Bread Upon the Waters: Federal Aid to the Maritime Industries.* Washington, D.C.: Brookings Institution, 1975, chapter 5.

This estimate is of the annual cost of cabotage to shipowners and users. The social cost is calculated as the differential between domestic and foreign shipbuilding and operating expenses. Historical differentials over the previous twenty years have been annualized and assumed to persist at the calculated level.

(e) Crandall, R., "Federal Government Initiatives to Reduce the Price Level," *Brookings Papers on Economic Activity,* no. 2. Washington, D.C.: Brookings Institution, 1978.

The author cites other existing studies on the impact of regulation on prices. The figures are "at best approximate and do not include a measure of deadweight loss nor reflect shifts among transportation." The author's figures fit within the ranges of other studies. Figures for 1976 were updated to 1977 by multiplying by the ratio of 1977 to 1976 operating revenues.

(f) Douglas, G. W. and Miller, James C., *Economic Regulation of Domestic Air Transport: Theory and Policy.* Washington, D.C.: Brookings Institution, 1974.

This estimate is of the difference between aggregate full cost fares and the lowest feasible aggregate costs achieved if the price-quality combination were competitively rather than regulatorily determined. This lowest feasible cost figure is determined by estimating the costs of unwanted service provided to justify high regulated fares. Figures for 1969 are inflated to 1977 estimates by multiplying by the ratio of 1977 to 1969 revenues.

(g) Comptroller General, General Accounting Office, "Lower Airline Costs Per Passenger Are Possible in the United States and Could Result in Lower Fares," CED-77-34, February 18, 1977.

Using a similar methodology to Douglas, the study finds that lower costs are attained in unregulated intrastate lines through high load factors, dense seating, and increased operating efficiency. This study does not estimate the deadweight loss or the value of additional service at lower fares.

(h) Comanor, W. and Mitchell, B., "The Costs of Planning the FCC and Cable Television," *Journal of Law and Economics* (April 1972): 177.

This estimate is of the deadweight welfare loss due to FCC pricing regulations. The figure is based upon the assumptions that the competitive price is equal to average cost, that the FCC price is $5.00 per month, and that demand elasticity is relatively low (as found in an earlier study.) The estimate is thus particularly sensitive to changes in the FCC-allowed price and increases in operating cost.

(i) Klass, M. W. and Weiss, L. W., *Study on Federal Regulation* for the Committee on Governmental Affairs, U.S. Senate, December 1978, volume 6, p. 64.

The authors cite the "implied" GAO estimate of what consumers would be willing to pay for a reduction in cable regulation.

(j) Smith, James, "The Equal Credit Opportunity Act of 1974: A Cost-Benefit Analysis." Paper presented at the Annual Meeting of the American Finance Association, September 1976 (mimeographed), pp. 1, 7, 8–18.

This estimate refers to the sum of the following costs necessary to comply with the Equal Credit Opportunity Act: legal, training, destruction of obsolete forms, reprogramming of computers, additional storage, printing, mailing, computer time, report writing, and customer service.

(k) Arthur Anderson and Company, *The Cost of Government Study for the Business Roundtable.* New York: Arthur Anderson and Company, March 1979.

This study employs the same methodology and conceptual basis as described in Appendix for table 2.4, note h.

(l) Ippolito, R. A. and Mason, R. T., *The Social Costs of Federal Regulation of Milk,* January 1976 (Mimeographed).

This estimate is of the costs of extra production due to high regulated prices, misallocation among consumers, and extra transportation and administration costs. The commonly cited figure of $300–400 million in social cost involves mostly transfers to producers and among producers.

(m) Arrow, K. and Kalt, J., *Petroleum Price Regulations: Should We Decontrol?* Washington, D.C.: American Enterprise Institute, 1979.

This is an estimate of dead weight loss due to price controls and the entitlement system. The figure is based on a producer response of 0.0 to 0.2 percent per year increase in output from existing fields for each 1 percent increase in price and a 0.5 percent per year increase in reserves for each 1 percent increase in price.

(n) MacAvoy, P. and Pindyck, R. S., *Price Controls and the Natural Gas Shortage.* Washington, D.C.: American Enterprise Institute for Public Policy Research, 1975.

This estimate is of the amount consumers would pay in 1978 for natural gas not produced due to artificially low prices mandated by the Federal Power Commission. The figure is derived from the author's model for energy supply and demand. The model's supply side forecasts production based upon cost, price, and risk factors. Demand is primarily determined by forecasts for economic growth.

(o) The totals in the range take the high and low from each source.

Table 2.7. Summary of Regulatory Cost Estimates

(a) The totals in the range take the high and low from each category of tables 2.4, 2.5, and 2.6. These totals exclude certain important programs, and the estimates often have quite different conceptual bases, as described above. In general, however, the costs of economic regulation are de lweight or efficiency costs, net of benefits.

The Measurement of the Indirect Effect of Regulation on Productivity

We provide here a description of the technique we have used to estimate the indirect effects of regulation on productivity.

Let output be given by a production function of the form, $X = F(L, L^*, E)$, where X = measured output, L = productive inputs, L^* = inputs used to abate pollution (direct inputs), and E = inputs used to overcome siting, legal, fuel-use, or other restrictions (indirect inputs).

Conventionally measured productivity is $X/(L + L^* + E)$; productivity subtracting inputs used to abate pollution (i.e., correcting for direct pollution-control inputs a la Denison) is $X/(L + E)$; and productivity correcting for all regulatory restrictions is X/L.

We have data on X and L; scanty data on L^*; but no data on E. Start with the hypothesis that the share of direct costs in output is highly correlated with the share of indirect costs in output (i.e., that E/X is closely related across industries to L^*/X). We then can regress the change in productivity growth before and after 1973 on L^*/X: $\Delta \text{Prod}_i = a + b (L^*/X)_i$, where ΔProd_i = change in percentage annual average productivity growth before and after 1973; $(L^*/X)_i$ = total pollution control cost as a percent of value of shipments in 1977; and i refers to fifty-eight four-digit manufacturing industries, excluding wet corn milling.[1] Results of the regression are given in the table below.

The estimated coefficient for the intercept is -1.01 (standard error of 0.39), which means that even if no industry had been required to curb its pollution after 1973, the annual rate of growth of productivity would

---

1. In this analysis, we omit wet-corn milling—a booming new industry that introduced a major new process of yielding high fructose corn syrups.

Estimated Impact of Pollution Control
Costs on Productivity Growth, 1947–79

Independent Variable	Estimated Coefficient	Standard Error	t-statistic
Intercept	−1.01	.39	−2.6
L^*/X	− .67	.57	−1.17
$R = .024$			

Standard error of regression = 2.41

still have been one percentage point less than it had been before 1973. The estimated coefficient for L^*/X (the ratio of total expenditure for pollution control to the value of output) is −0.67 (standard error of 0.57)—the appropriate sign but not an extraordinarily well-determined coefficient.

If further unexplained determinants of productivity growth are uncorrelated with L^*/X, we can use the regression results to determine the relation between direct and indirect impacts on productivity. This is calculated as follows: an increase in L^* equal to 1 percent of the total value of shipments over a five year period should lower measured productivity growth—(i.e., growth in $X/(L+L^*+E)$—by 0.2 percent per annum. If direct costs are one-half of indirect costs, if L^*/X and E/X are perfectly correlated, and if L^* and E^* are initially small, then the coefficient of productivity growth on the share of direct pollution abatement costs should be 0.6 rather than 0.2.

In fact, our point estimate of the coefficient of direct costs is 0.67—which is approximately three times larger than the coefficient should be for direct costs alone. Such a coefficient implies that indirect costs are about two times direct costs; or else that direct costs are understated; or else that spurious correlations have biased the estimates.

As a final note it should be stated that the statistical determination of the coefficient is poor and that the coefficient could easily be two times larger than our best guess, or essentially zero, given the data we have gathered.

APPENDIX C

Balancing of Costs and Benefits in Regulatory Statutes

Listed below are statutes that fall in each of the three categories identified in the text: those prohibiting, permitting, and requiring the relevant agency to balance costs against benefits in making regulatory decisions. The list is not exhaustive and has been prepared for illustrative purposes only.

I. Statutes Prohibiting Balancing
- A. Delaney Clause of the Food, Drug and Cosmetic Act (21 U.S.C. § 376(b)(5) and 21 U.S.C. § 348(C)(3)(A))—food additives that are found by the FDA "to induce cancer in man or animal" must be banned (regardless of costs or offsetting health-related or economic benefits).
- B. National primary ambient air quality standards set under the Clean Air Act (42 U.S. C. § 7409(b)(1))—to be set "requisite to protect the public health," allowing an "adequate margin of safety."
- C. "Fishable/Swimmable" criteria under the Clean Water Act (33 U.S.C. § 1251(a)(2))—water quality goal to be achieved by 1983 must provide "for the protection and propagation of fish, shellfish, and wildlife . . ." wherever "attainable."

II. Statutes Permitting Balancing
The statutes in this category permit costs and benefits to be taken into account to varying degrees.
- A. Toxic substance standards set under the Occupational Safety and Health Act (29 U.S.C. § 655(b) (5))—standards to be set such that "*to the extent feasible* . . . no employee will suffer

material impairment of health or functional capacity'' (emphasis added); the Supreme Court has held that costs can be considered only in connection with the ''feasibility'' of the standards governing exposure to toxic substances. *American Textile Manufacturers Institute, Inc.* v. *Donovan*, 452 U.S. 490 (1981).

B. Regulation of nuclear power activities under the Atomic Energy Act of 1954, as amended (42 U.S.C. § 2011 *et seq.*) and the Energy Reorganization Act of 1974 (42 U.S.C. § 5801 *et seq.*)—although these acts do not explicitly require a balancing of costs and benefits in setting standards on nuclear power activities and for licensing reactors, the NRC has interpreted the statutes to permit such balancing.

C. Technology-based effluent standards of the Clean Water Act (33 U.S.C. § 1251 *et seq.*)—water effluent standards for 1977 to be based on ''best practicable'' technology (BPT); for 1987 on the ''best available technology'' (BAT). Benefits and costs of effluent standards are clearly to be balanced in setting the BPT standards, 33 U.S.C. § 1314(b)(1); the effect of balancing is much more restricted in setting the BAT standards, 33 U.S.C. § 1314(b)(2). See discussion in *EPA* v. *National Crushed Stone Association*, 101 S. Ct. 295 (1980).

III. Statutes Requiring Balancing

A. Fuel economy standards under the National Energy Policy Conservation Act (15 U.S.C. § 2002(e))—directs the Secretary (Transportation) to take into account ''technological feasibility,'' ''economic practicability,'' and energy-conservation concerns in setting the ''maximum feasible average fuel economy.''

B. New source performance standards under the Clean Air Act (42 U.S.C. § 7411(a)(1))—directs the EPA Administrator to set new source emission standards applicable to ''the best system of continuous emission reduction . . . *(taking into consideration the cost of achieving such emission reduction, and any nonair quality health and environmental impact and energy requirements)*'' (emphasis added).

C. Toxic Substances Control Act (15 U.S.C. § 2605(a))—regulates the manufacture of toxic substances that present an *''unreasonable risk* of injury to the health or the environment'' (emphasis added) (generally regarded to require balancing).

D. Federal Environmental Pesticide Control Act (7 U.S.C. § 136(bb), 136(a)(c)(5)(A-D))—bans pesticides that pose "any unreasonable risk to man or the environment *taking into account the economic, social, and environmental costs of the pesticide*" (emphasis added).

E. Consumer Product Safety Act (15 U.S.C. § 2056(a)—directs the promulgation of standards that are "reasonably necessary to prevent or reduce an unreasonable risk of injury associated with a [consumer] product" (held to require balancing in *Aqua Slide N' Dive* v. *Consumer Product Safety*, 569 F.2d 831 (5th Cir. 1978)).

F. Motor Vehicle Safety Standards (15 U.S.C. § 1392)—in setting such standards, the Secretary (Transportation) shall consider, among other things, "whether any such proposed standard is reasonable, practicable, and appropriate for the particular type of motor vehicle."

Index

195